OXFORD
PHOTO
DICTIONARY

INGLESE–ITALIANO

Oxford University Press

Oxford University Press
Great Clarendon Street, Oxford OX2 6DP

Oxford New York

Athens Auckland Bangkok Bogotá Buenos Aires
Calcutta Cape Town Chennai Dar es Salaam
Delhi Florence Hong Kong Istanbul Karachi
Kuala Lumpur Madrid Melbourne Mexico City
Mumbai Nairobi Paris São Paulo Singapore
Taipei Tokyo Toronto Warsaw

and associated companies in
Berlin Ibadan

Oxford and Oxford English are trade marks of
Oxford University Press

ISBN 0 19 431371 9

Italian edition © Oxford University Press 1992

First published 1992
Fifth impression 1999

Editor: Jane Taylor

Printed in Hong Kong

Acknowledgements

Location and studio photography by: Graham Alder, Chris
Andrews, Martyn Chillmaid, Nigel Cull, Nick Fogden,
Paul Freestone, Gareth Jones, Mark Mason.

**The publishers would like to thank the following for
permission to reproduce photographs:** ABI Caravans Ltd;
Allsport (UK) Ltd/B Asset, S Bruty, R Cheyne, T Duffy,
S Dunn, J Gichigi, J Hayt, B Hazelton, H Heiderman,
J Loubat, A Murrell, J Nicholson, M Powell, P Rondeau,
H Stein; Animal Photography/S Thompson, R Willbie;
Ardea London Ltd/D Avon, I Beames, L Beames,
J Clegg, E Dragesco, M England, J Ferrero, K Fink,
D Greenslade, A Lindau, J Mason, E Mickleburgh,
P Morris, S Roberts, R & V Taylor, A Weaving, W Weisser;
Art Directors Photo Library/S Grant; Associated Sports
Photography; Clive Barda; Barnaby's Picture Library;
J Allan Cash Ltd; Bruce Coleman Ltd/J Anthony, E & B
Bauer, J Burton, M Dohrn, J Foot, N Fox-Davies,
M Kahl, G Langsbury, W Layer, G McCarthy, M Price,
A Purcell, H Reinhard, K Taylor, N Tomalin,
R Wilmshurst; Colorsport/Compoint; Cotswold Wildlife
Park; Cunard Line Ltd; Mary Evans Picture Library; Fiat
Fork Lift Trucks; Michael Fogden; Ford Motor Company
Ltd; Robert Harding Picture Library/Griffiths, G Renner;
Eric Hoskin/W Pitt; Hovertravel Ltd; Libby Howells; The
Hutchison Library/M Scorer; Rob Judges; Landscape
Only; Frank Lane Picture Agency/A Albinger, R Jones,
Silvestris, M Thomas, L West; Leyland Daf; London
Tourist Board; Mazda Cars (UK) Ltd; Metropolitan
Police; National Motor Museum, Beaulieu; Oxford
Scientific Films Stills/S Dalton, L Lauber, M Leach,
Partridge Films Ltd, Presstige Pictures, R Redfern,
F Skibbe, G Wren; Planet Earth Pictures/Seaphot/M Clay,
W Deas, D George, J George, K Lucas, J Lythgoe,
N Middleton, J Scott, J Watt; Renault UK Ltd; Rex
Features Ltd/N Jorgensen, J Tarrant; Rover Cars;
RSPB/G Downey, P Perfect, M Richards; Science Photo
Library/T Beddow, M Bond, Dr J Burgess, D Campione,
M Dohrn, T Fearon-Jones, V Fleming, NASA, S Patel,
R Royer, St Bartholomew's Hospital, J Sanford,
S Stammers, J Stevenson, S Terry; Shell UK Ltd;
Spectrum Colour Library; Swift Picture Library/T
Dressler, M Mockler; Toleman Automotive Ltd; Trust
House Forte; Wedgewood; World Pictures; Zefa/D
Cattani, Damm, D Davies, Goebel, C Krebs, R Maylander,
K Oster, J Pfaff, A Roberts, Rosenfeld, Selitsch.

**The publishers would like to thank the following for their
help and assistance:** Abingdon Hospital; Abingdon
Surgery; Russell Acott Ltd; Apollo Theatre; B & L
Mechanical Services, Eynsham; Douglas Bader Sports
Centre, St Edward's School; Barclays Bank; BBC Radio
Oxford; The Bear & Ragged Staff, Cumnor; H C Biggers,
Eynsham; Boswells of Oxford; Bournemouth
International Airport; British Rail; Cassington Builders
Ltd; Cheney School; Cherwell School; City Camera
Exchange, Brighton; Comet; Daisies, Oxford; Early
Learning Centre; Education & Sci Products Ltd; Elmer
Cotton Sports, Oxford; Eynsham Car Repairs; Faulkner &
Sons Ltd; For Eyes; Phylis Goodman Ltd, Eynsham;
Habitat Designs Ltd; W R Hammond & Son Ltd,
Eynsham; Hartford Motors Ltd; Headington Sports;
Heather's Delicatessen, Hove; Hove Delicatessen;
Inshape Body Studios Ltd; Johnsons of Oxford;
Littlewoods PLC; London Underground Ltd; Malin
Farms, Eynsham; P J Meagher, Eynsham; John Menzies
Ltd; North Kidlington Primary School; Ocean Village
Marina, Marina Developments PLC; Nigel Olesen BDS;
Options Hair Studio, Eynsham; Oxford Despatch; Oxford
Royal Mail & Post Office Counters; Paramount Sewing
Machines; Parkwood Veterinary Group; Payless DIY;
Phoenix One & Two; Qualifruit; Red Funnel Isle of Wight
Ferries; SS Mary & John School; Southampton Eastleigh
Airport; Stanhope Wilkinson Associates, Eynsham;
Summertown Travel; Texas Homecare, Oxford; Paul
Thomas; Richard Walton, Eynsham; Warlands, Cycle
Agents; Welsh National Opera; Western Newsagents,
Hove; Chris Yapp Consultants Ltd.

Indice

Family Relationships <small>page 1</small>

La famiglia di John	John's Family
nonna	**1** grandmother
nonno	**2** grandfather
zia	**3** aunt
zio	**4** uncle
madre	**5** mother
padre	**6** father
suocero	**7** father-in-law
suocera	**8** mother-in-law
cugino/a	**9** cousin
cognato	**10** brother-in-law
sorella	**11** sister
moglie	**12** wife
cognata	**13** sister-in-law
nipote	**14** niece
nipote	**15** nephew
figlio	**16** son
figlia	**17** daughter

John è il marito di Ann.	**18** John is Ann's **husband.**
Tom e Lisa sono i figli di John e Ann.	**19** Tom and Lisa are John and Ann's **children.**
John e Ann sono i genitori di Tom e Lisa.	**20** John and Ann are Tom and Lisa's **parents.**
Mary e Bob Cox e Ian e Jane Hill sono i nonni di Tom e Lisa.	**21** Mary and Bob Cox and Ian and Jane Hill are Tom and Lisa's **grandparents.**
Tom è il loro nipote.	**22** Tom is their **grandson.**
Lisa è la loro nipote.	**23** Lisa is their **granddaughter.**

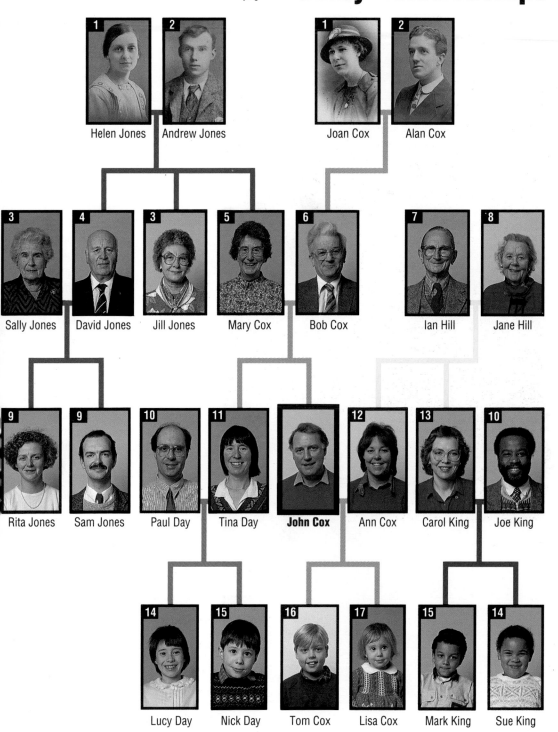

The Human Body 1

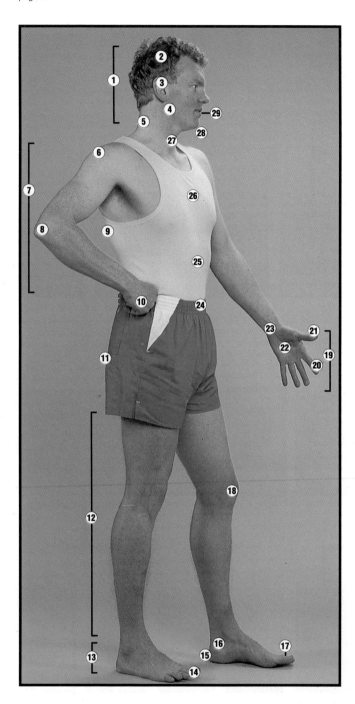

testa	**1** head
capelli	**2** hair
orecchio	**3** ear
mascella/mandibola	**4** jaw
collo	**5** neck
spalla	**6** shoulder
braccio	**7** arm
gomito	**8** elbow
schiena	**9** back
pugno	**10** fist
natiche/sedere	**11** buttocks/bottom
gamba	**12** leg
piede	**13** foot
dito del piede	**14** toe
tallone	**15** heel
caviglia	**16** ankle
unghia	**17** nail
ginocchio	**18** knee
mano	**19** hand
dito	**20** finger
pollice	**21** thumb
palmo	**22** palm
polso	**23** wrist
vita/cintura	**24** waist
stomaco	**25** stomach
petto	**26** chest
gola	**27** throat
mento	**28** chin
bocca	**29** mouth

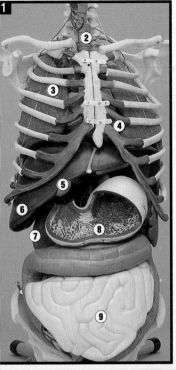

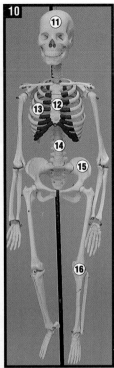

organi interni	**1**	internal organs
trachea	**2**	trachea/windpipe
polmone	**3**	lung
cuore	**4**	heart
cistifellea	**5**	gall-bladder
fegato	**6**	liver
rene	**7**	kidney
stomaco	**8**	stomach
intestino	**9**	intestines
scheletro	**10**	skeleton
cranio	**11**	skull
sterno	**12**	breastbone
costola	**13**	rib
spina dorsale	**14**	spine/backbone
bacino/osso iliaco	**15**	pelvis/hip-bone
rotula	**16**	kneecap

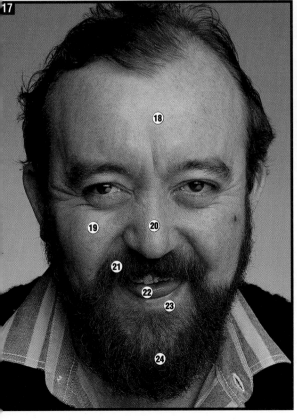

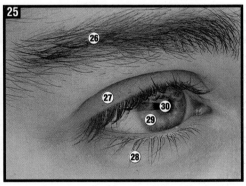

faccia/viso	**17**	face
fronte	**18**	forehead
guancia	**19**	cheek
naso	**20**	nose
baffi	**21**	moustache
lingua	**22**	tongue
labbro	**23**	lip
barba	**24**	beard
occhio	**25**	eye
sopracciglio	**26**	eyebrow
palpebra	**27**	eyelid
ciglio	**28**	eyelash
iride	**29**	iris
pupilla	**30**	pupil

Physical Description

Età	Age
bambino/a	**1** baby
bambino	**2** child/(young) boy
adolescente/ragazza	**3** teenager/teenage gi
adulta/donna	**4** adult/woman
adulto/uomo	**5** adult/man
anziano	**6** elderly (*or* old) man
Capelli	**Hair**
testa calva	**7** bald head
corti lisci scuri	**8** short straight dark
corti lisci biondi	**9** short straight fair
corti ricci/riccioluti	**10** short curly
corti ondulati	**11** short wavy
lunghi rossi	**12** long red
	(*Brit also* ginger)
coda di cavallo	**13** pony tail
frangia	**14** fringe (*US* bangs)
lunghi biondi	**15** long blonde
riga	**16** parting (*US* part)
treccia	**17** plait (*US* braid)
alto	**18** tall
basso	**19** short
magro	**20** thin
grasso	**21** fat

What's the matter?

page 6

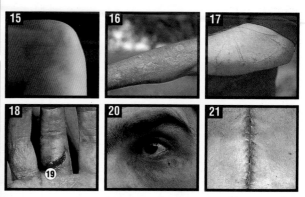

Ha sete.	**1** She's thirsty.
Ha fame.	**2** She's hungry.
È stanca.	**3** She's tired.
Ha mal di denti.	**4** She's got toothache.
	(*US* She has a toothache.)
Ha mal di stomaco/pancia.	**5** She's got stomach-ache.
	(*US* She has a stomachache.)
Ha mal di testa.	**6** She's got a headache.
	(*US* She has a headache.)
Ha il raffreddore.	**7** He's got a cold.
	(*US* He has a cold.)
Ha mal di gola.	**8** He's got a sore throat.
	(*US* He has a sore throat.)
Ha la tosse.	**9** He's got a cough.
	(*US* He has a cough.)
Ha la febbre.	**10** He's got a temperature.
	(*US* He has a temperature.)
Incidenti/infortuni	**Accidents**
È caduto.	**11** He's fallen over.
	(*US* He fell over.)
Si è fatto male alla gamba.	**12** He's hurt his leg.
	(*US* He hurt his leg.)
Si è rotta la gamba.	**13** She's broken her leg.
	(*US* She broke her leg.)
Si è slogata la caviglia.	**14** She's sprained her ankle.
	(*US* She sprained her ankle.)
livido	**15** bruise
scottatura	**16** sunburn
graffio	**17** scratch
taglio/ferita	**18** cut
sangue	**19** blood
occhio pesto	**20** black eye
cicatrice	**21** scar

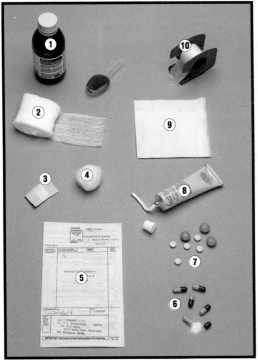

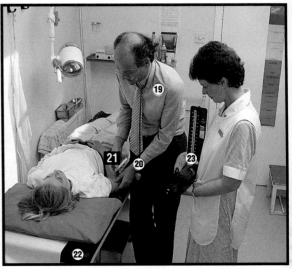

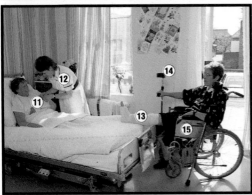

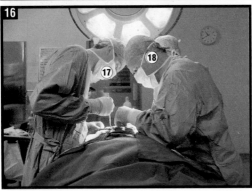

medicina	**1**	medicine
benda/fascia	**2**	bandage
cerotto	**3**	(sticking-)plaster (*US* Band-Aid)
cotone idrofilo/ovatta	**4**	cotton wool (*US* cotton ball)
ricetta medica	**5**	prescription
capsula	**6**	capsule
pastiglia/compressa	**7**	pill/tablet
pomata	**8**	ointment
garza	**9**	gauze pad
cerotto adesivo	**10**	adhesive tape
Reparto di ospedale		**Hospital Ward** (***US also*** **Hospital Room**)
benda	**11**	sling
infermiera	**12**	nurse
ingessatura/gesso	**13**	plaster cast (*US* cast)
stampella	**14**	crutch
sedia a rotelle/carrozzella	**15**	wheelchair
Operazione		**Operation**
sala operatoria	**16**	operating theatre (*US* operating room)
maschera	**17**	mask
chirurgo	**18**	surgeon
Ambulatorio medico		**Doctor's Surgery** (***US*** **Doctor's Office**)
dottore/medico	**19**	doctor
stetoscopio	**20**	stethoscope
iniezione/puntura	**21**	injection
lettino	**22**	examination couch (*US* examining table/ examination table)
misuratore di pressione	**23**	blood pressure gauge

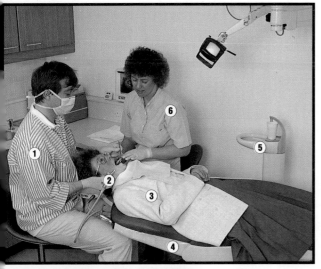

Dal dentista **At the Dentist's**

dentista	**1**	dentist
trapano	**2**	drill
paziente	**3**	patient
poltrona	**4**	dentist's chair
lavabo	**5**	basin
assistente del dentista	**6**	dental nurse
		(*US* dental assistant)
gengiva	**7**	gum
dente	**8**	tooth
otturazione	**9**	filling
radiografia	**10**	X-ray (*also* x-ray)
denti anteriori	**11**	front teeth
denti posteriori	**12**	back teeth

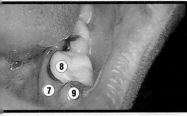

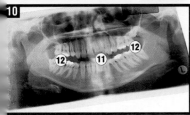

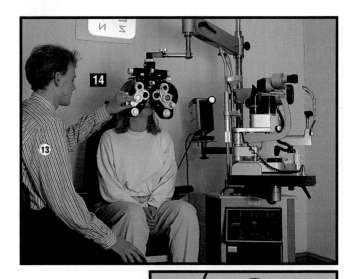

Dall'oculista **At the Optician's**

oculista	**13**	optician
controllo della vista	**14**	eye test
(paio di) occhiali	**15**	(pair of) glasses
lente	**16**	lens
ponticello	**17**	bridge
montatura	**18**	frame
custodia per occhiali	**19**	glasses case
		(*US also* eyeglass case)
lente a contatto	**20**	contact lens
collirio/gocce per gli occhi	**21**	eye drops
soluzione detergente per lenti a contatto	**22**	contact lens cleaner

Describing Clothes

page 9

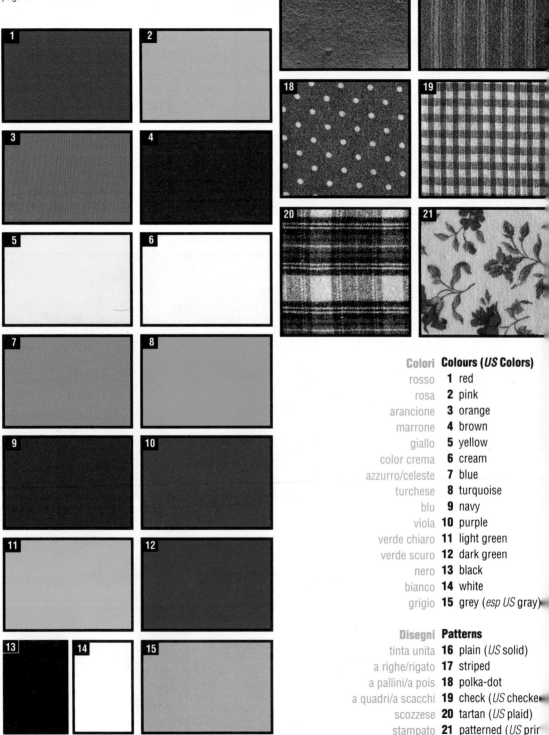

Colori	Colours (*US* Colors)
rosso	**1** red
rosa	**2** pink
arancione	**3** orange
marrone	**4** brown
giallo	**5** yellow
color crema	**6** cream
azzurro/celeste	**7** blue
turchese	**8** turquoise
blu	**9** navy
viola	**10** purple
verde chiaro	**11** light green
verde scuro	**12** dark green
nero	**13** black
bianco	**14** white
grigio	**15** grey (*esp US* gray)

Disegni	Patterns
tinta unita	**16** plain (*US* solid)
a righe/rigato	**17** striped
a pallini/a pois	**18** polka-dot
a quadri/a scacchi	**19** check (*US* checke
scozzese	**20** tartan (*US* plaid)
stampato	**21** patterned (*US* prir

divisa scolastica	1	school uniform
berretto	2	cap
blazer/giacca	3	blazer
pantaloni/calzoni	4	trousers (*US* pants)
T-shirt/maglietta	5	T-shirt
maglione	6	sweater
jeans	7	jeans
giaccone	8	jacket
camicetta	9	blouse
borsetta	10	handbag (*US also* purse)
gonna	11	skirt
cartella	12	briefcase
stivale	13	boot
sciarpa	14	scarf
guanto	15	glove
ombrello	16	umbrella
cappotto	17	coat
completo	18	suit
camicia	19	shirt
cravatta	20	tie
fazzoletto	21	handkerchief
impermeabile	22	raincoat
scarpa	23	shoe

Clothes 2 page 11

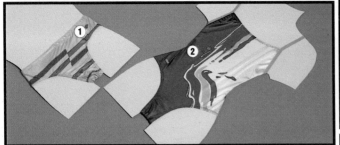

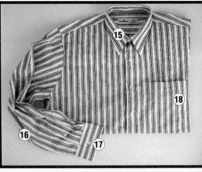

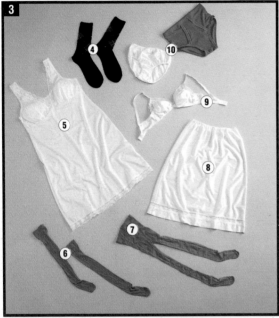

costume da bagno	**1**	swimming-trunks (*US* bathing suit)
costume da bagno	**2**	swimsuit (*US* bathing suit)
biancheria intima	**3**	underwear
calzini	**4**	socks
sottoveste	**5**	full slip
calze	**6**	stockings
collant	**7**	tights (*US* pantyhose)
sottogonna	**8**	half slip
reggiseno	**9**	bra
mutande	**10**	pants (*US* underpants)
camicia da notte	**11**	night-dress (*US* nightgown)
pantofola	**12**	slipper
vestaglia	**13**	dressing gown (*US* robe)
pigiama	**14**	pyjamas (*US* pajamas)
colletto	**15**	collar
manica	**16**	sleeve
polsino	**17**	cuff
tasca	**18**	pocket
fibbia	**19**	buckle
tacco	**20**	heel
portafoglio	**21**	wallet
borsellino/portamonete	**22**	purse (*US* wallet)
laccio da scarpe	**23**	shoelace

pilota di macchine da corsa	**1**	racing driver (*US* race car driver)
casco	**2**	helmet
tuta da ginnastica	**3**	track suit (*US also* jogging suit)
scarpa da ginnastica	**4**	trainer (*US* sneaker)
zingara	**5**	gypsy
foulard	**6**	scarf
cardigan/giacca di lana	**7**	cardigan
sandalo	**8**	sandal
pugile	**9**	boxer
canottiera	**10**	vest (*US* tank top)
cintura	**11**	belt
calzoncini/calzoni corti	**12**	shorts
mostro	**13**	monster
felpa	**14**	sweatshirt
orologio da polso	**15**	watch
strega	**16**	witch
cappello	**17**	hat
occhiali da sole	**18**	sun-glasses
vestito	**19**	dress
trucco	**20**	make-up
rossetto	**21**	lipstick

Gioielli Jewellery (*esp US* Jewelry)

spilla	**22**	brooch (*US* pin)
braccialetto	**23**	bracelet
anello	**24**	ring
catena	**25**	chain
collana	**26**	necklace
orecchino	**27**	earring

Buildings 1
 page 13

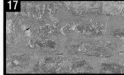

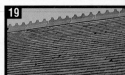

casa a schiera	**1**	terraced house (*US* town house)
tetto di tegole	**2**	slate roof
cassetta dei fiori	**3**	window-box
battente	**4**	knocker
cassetta della posta	**5**	letter-box (*US* mailbox)
soglia	**6**	doorstep
muro di mattoni	**7**	brick wall
finestra scorrevole	**8**	sash window
finestra del seminterrato	**9**	basement window
palazzo/condominio	**10**	block of flats (*US* apartment house)
ultimo piano	**11**	top floor
balcone/terrazzo	**12**	balcony
primo piano	**13**	first floor (*US* second floor)
piano terra	**14**	ground floor (*US also* first floor)
parcheggio	**15**	car-park (*US* parking lot)
Materiali per costruzioni		**Building Materials**
mattone	**16**	brick
pietra	**17**	stone
calcestruzzo/cemento	**18**	concrete
tegola	**19**	tile
tegola d'ardesia	**20**	slate
copertura di paglia	**21**	thatch
legno	**22**	wood
vetro	**23**	glass

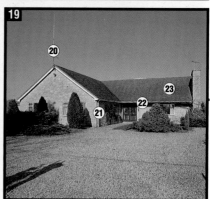

casa singola	**1**	detached house (*US* one-family house)
garage	**2**	garage
porta d'entrata	**3**	front door
colonna/pilastro	**4**	pillar
imposta	**5**	shutter
casa bifamiliare	**6**	semi-detached house (*US* two-family house)
camino	**7**	chimney
finestra	**8**	window
davanzale	**9**	window-sill/window-ledge
arco	**10**	arch
bovindo	**11**	bay window
muro di cemento	**12**	concrete wall

villino	**13**	cottage
tetto di paglia	**14**	thatched roof
abbaino	**15**	dormer
portico	**16**	porch
cancello di legno	**17**	wooden gate
muro di pietra	**18**	stone wall
bungalow	**19**	bungalow (*US* ranch house)
antenna TV	**20**	TV aerial (*US* antenna)
tubo di scolo	**21**	drainpipe
grondaia	**22**	gutter
tetto di tegole	**23**	tiled roof

The Dining-room

specchio	**1** mirror		bicchiere	**14** glass
parete	**2** wall		sale	**15** salt
candela	**3** candle		pepe	**16** pepper
termosifone/radiatore	**4** radiator		brocca	**17** jug (*US* pitcher)
coperchio	**5** lid		credenza	**18** sideboard (*US* buffet)
terrina	**6** dish		cassetto	**19** drawer
tovagliolo	**7** napkin		vaso	**20** vase
tovaglia	**8** table-cloth		caffettiera	**21** coffee-pot
piatto	**9** plate		lampada da tavolo	**22** lamp
coltello	**10** knife		paralume	**23** lampshade
cucchiaio	**11** spoon		cornice	**24** frame
forchetta	**12** fork		dipinto/quadro	**25** painting
piatto fondo	**13** bowl		orologio da muro	**26** clock

soffitto	**1** ceiling	piattino	**13** saucer
mensola del camino	**2** mantelpiece (*US* mantel)	tazza	**14** cup
caminetto	**3** fireplace	cucchiaino	**15** teaspoon
fuoco	**4** fire	cestino	**16** waste-paper basket
ciocco/ceppo	**5** log	divano/sofà	**17** sofa (*esp US* couch)
tappeto	**6** rug	cuscino	**18** cushion
moquette	**7** carpet	pianta	**19** plant
tavolino da salotto	**8** coffee-table	tende	**20** curtains (*US* drapes)
telecomando	**9** remote control	mobile a muro	**21** wall unit
biscottiera	**10** biscuit tin (*US* cookie tin)	poltrona	**22** armchair
teiera	**11** teapot	televisione	**23** television/TV
vassoio	**12** tray	videoregistratore	**24** video cassette recorder/VCR

The Bathroom

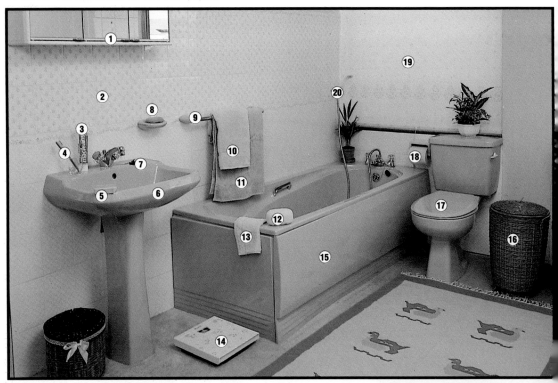

armadietto	**1** bathroom cabinet (*US* medicine chest/cabinet)
piastrella	**2** tile
tubo di dentifricio	**3** tube of toothpaste
spazzolino da denti	**4** toothbrush
spazzolino da unghie	**5** nail-brush
lavandino/lavabo	**6** wash-basin (*US* sink)
tappo	**7** plug (*US* stopper)
saponetta	**8** bar of soap
portasciugamano	**9** towel-rail (*US* towel rack)
asciugamano	**10** hand-towel
telo da bagno	**11** bath-towel
spugna	**12** sponge
salvietta	**13** flannel (*US* washcloth)
bilancia	**14** (bathroom) scales (*US* scale)
vasca da bagno	**15** bath (*US* bathtub)
cesto per il bucato	**16** laundry basket (*US* hamper)
water	**17** toilet
carta igienica	**18** toilet paper
tenda a rullo	**19** blind (*US* shade)
doccia	**20** shower

dopobarba	**21** aftershave (*US* after-shave lotion)
rasoio elettrico	**22** electric razor
rasoio	**23** razor
lametta	**24** razor-blade
schiuma da barba	**25** shaving-foam (*US* shaving cream)
shampoo	**26** shampoo
pettine	**27** comb
borotalco/talco	**28** talcum powder (*also* talc

toilette	**1**	dressing table (*US* dresser)
biancheria da letto	**2**	bed-linen
letto	**3**	bed
copriletto	**4**	bedspread
coperta	**5**	blanket
lenzuolo	**6**	sheet
federa	**7**	pillowcase
spazzola per capelli	**8**	hairbrush
scatola di fazzolettini	**9**	box of tissues
comodino	**10**	bedside cabinet (*US* night table)
materasso	**11**	mattress
guanciale	**12**	pillow
testata	**13**	headboard
sveglia	**14**	alarm clock
poster/manifesto	**15**	poster
lampada	**16**	light
armadio	**17**	wardrobe (*US* closet)
portabiti/gruccia	**18**	coat-hanger (*esp US* hanger)
cassettiera	**19**	chest of drawers (*US also* bureau)
asciugacapelli/fon	**20**	hair-drier (*or* hair-dryer)

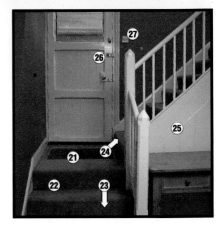

zerbino	**21**	doormat
scalino/gradino	**22**	stair (*esp US* step)
di sotto/dabbasso	**23**	downstairs
di sopra/al piano superiore	**24**	upstairs
scala	**25**	staircase
serratura	**26**	lock
interruttore	**27**	light switch

detergente/detersivo	**1** detergent		ferro da stiro	**13** iron
lavandino/acquaio	**2** sink		panno per la polvere	**14** duster (*US* dust cloth)
lavatrice	**3** washing-machine		lampadina	**15** light-bulb
paletta	**4** dustpan		gancio	**16** hook
spazzola	**5** brush		torcia	**17** torch (*US* flashlight)
secchio	**6** bucket (*esp US* pail)		spazzola/bruschino	**18** scrubbing-brush
aspirapolvere	**7** vacuum cleaner			(*US* scrub brush)
	(*Brit also* Hoover)		rubinetto dell'acqua fredda	**19** cold(-water) tap
mocio Vileda	**8** mop			(*US* cold water faucet)
asse da stiro	**9** ironing-board		rubinetto dell'acqua calda	**20** hot(-water) tap
pinza da bucato/molletta	**10** clothes-peg (*US* clothespin)			(*US* hot water faucet)
filo	**11** flex (*esp US* cord)		presa di corrente	**21** socket (*US also* outlet)
spina	**12** plug		corda per stendere il bucato	**22** clothes-line

casseruola	**1** casserole		freezer/congelatore	**15** freezer
setaccio	**2** sieve (*esp US* strainer)		tazza	**16** mug
ciotola/terrina	**3** mixing bowl		tostapane	**17** toaster
libro di cucina	**4** cookery book (*US* cookbook)		tagliere	**18** breadboard
detersivo per piatti	**5** washing-up liquid			(*US* cutting board)
	(*US* dishwashing liquid)		bollitore	**19** kettle
spugna abrasiva	**6** scourer (*US* scouring pad)			(*US* electric teakettle)
canovaccio/strofinaccio	**7** tea towel (*US* dish towel)		credenza	**20** cupboard (*esp US* cabinet)
sbattitore elettrico	**8** mixer		guanto da forno	**21** oven glove (*US* pot holder)
colapasta	**9** colander		forno	**22** oven
apriscatole	**10** tin-opener (*US* can opener)		ripiano/mensola	**23** shelf
mestolo	**11** ladle		padella	**24** frying-pan
mattarello	**12** rolling-pin		robot di cucina	**25** food processor
piano di lavoro	**13** work surface (*US* counter)		pentola	**26** saucepan/pot
frigorifero	**14** fridge (*esp US* refrigerator)		fornello	**27** burner

Tools

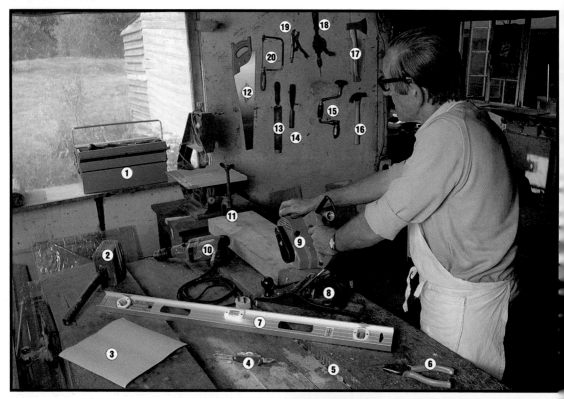

cassetta degli attrezzi	**1** tool-box
martello di legno	**2** mallet
carta vetrata	**3** sandpaper
temperino	**4** penknife (*esp US* pocketknife)
banco da lavoro	**5** workbench
pinze	**6** pliers
livella a bolla d'aria	**7** spirit-level (*US* level)
pialla	**8** plane
sega elettrica	**9** power saw
trapano elettrico	**10** electric drill
morsa	**11** vice (*US* vise)
sega a mano	**12** handsaw (*esp US* saw)
lima	**13** file
scalpello/cesello	**14** chisel
trapano a manubrio	**15** brace
martello	**16** hammer
accetta	**17** hatchet
trapano a mano	**18** hand drill
chiave a rollino	**19** wrench
seghetto	**20** coping saw

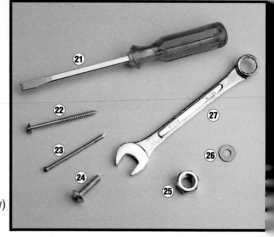

cacciavite	**21** screwdriver
vite	**22** screw
chiodo	**23** nail
bullone	**24** bolt
dado	**25** nut
rondella	**26** washer
chiave	**27** spanner (*US* wrench)

giardino dietro la casa	**1**	back garden (*US* backyard)
altalena	**2**	swing
erba/prato	**3**	grass/lawn
albero	**4**	tree
tosaerba	**5**	lawnmower
annaffiatoio	**6**	watering-can
rastrello	**7**	rake
cesoie/forbici	**8**	shears
cespuglio	**9**	bush
vaso da fiori	**10**	flowerpot
patio	**11**	patio
paletta da giardiniere	**12**	trowel
scopa	**13**	broom
panchina	**14**	bench
staccionata/recinzione	**15**	fence
barbecue	**16**	barbecue
carriola	**17**	wheelbarrow
forca	**18**	fork
vanga/pala	**19**	spade
bidone per le immondizie	**20**	dustbin
		(*US* garbage can)

giardino davanti alla casa	**21**	front garden
		(*US* front yard)
cancello	**22**	gate
vialetto	**23**	path (*US* front walk)
aiuola	**24**	flower-bed
muro	**25**	wall
viale d'accesso al garage	**26**	drive (*US* driveway)
siepe	**27**	hedge

Verdura	**Vegetables**		zucchino	**12** courgette (*US* zucchini)
banco/bancarella	**1** market stall (*US* stand)		crescione d'acqua	**13** watercress
aglio	**2** garlic		carota	**14** carrot
peperone verde	**3** green pepper		cavoletto di Bruxelles	**15** Brussels sprout
cavolfiore	**4** cauliflower			(*US* brussels sprout)
asparagi	**5** asparagus		sedano	**16** celery
ravanello	**6** radish		broccolo	**17** broccoli
lattuga/insalata	**7** lettuce		rapa	**18** turnip
barbabietola	**8** beetroot (*US* beet)		pomodoro	**19** tomato
patata	**9** potato		melanzana	**20** aubergine (*US* eggplant)
cetriolo	**10** cucumber		verza/cavolo	**21** cabbage
cipolla	**11** onion		sacchetto di carta	**22** paper bag

Frutta	**Fruit**
melone	**1** melon
cestino di fragole	**2** punnet of strawberries
	(*US* basket of strawberries)
casco di banane	**3** bunch of bananas
mela	**4** apple
nocciolina americana/arachide	**5** peanut
limone	**6** lemon
noce di cocco	**7** coconut
ananas	**8** pineapple
arancia	**9** orange
grappolo d'uva	**10** bunch of grapes
pesca	**11** peach
sacchetto di nocciole	**12** bag of nuts
avocado	**13** avocado
papaia	**14** pawpaw (*esp US* papaya)
litchi	**15** lychee (*also* litchi)
pera	**16** pear
limetta	**17** lime
kiwi	**18** kiwi fruit
mango	**19** mango
susina	**20** plum
pompelmo	**21** grapefruit
pila di cestini	**22** stack of baskets

At the Florist's page 25

pino	**1** pine tree (*also* Christmas tree)		crisantemo	**15** chrysanthemum
tronco	**2** trunk		palma	**16** palm
radici	**3** roots		rosa	**17** rose
petalo	**4** petal		orchidea	**18** orchid
felce	**5** fern		stelo/gambo	**19** stem
cesto	**6** basket		fresia	**20** freesia
ramo	**7** branch		cactus	**21** cactus
corteccia	**8** bark		pigna	**22** pine cone
mazzo di fiori secchi	**9** bunch of dried flowers		margherita	**23** daisy
composizione di fiori secchi	**10** dried flower arrangement		garofano	**24** carnation
foglia	**11** leaf		tulipano	**25** tulip
bonsai	**12** bonsai		giglio	**26** lily
bulbo	**13** bulb		bocciolo	**27** bud
narciso	**14** daffodil		iris	**28** iris

Dolciumi	Confectionery (*US* Candy)
scatola di cioccolatini	**9** box of chocolates (*US* box of chocolate)
sacchetto di caramelle	**10** bag of sweets (*US* bag of candy)
tavoletta di cioccolata	**11** bar of chocolate
confezione doppia	**12** twin-pack
confezione tripla	**13** triple-pack
pacchetto di caramelle	**14** packet of sweets (*US* pack of candy)
pacchetto di caramelle	**15** packet of sweets (*US* roll of candy)
sacchetto di patatine	**16** packet of crisps (*US* bag of potato chips)
cioccolata	**17** chocolate
dolciumi	**18** sweets (*US* candy)
patatine fritte	**19** crisps (*US* potato chips)

Cancelleria	Stationery
rotolo di nastro adesivo	**1** reel of Sellotape (*US* roll of Scotch tape)
gomitolo di spago	**2** ball of string
pacco di buste	**3** packet of envelopes (*US* pack of envelopes)
carta da lettere	**4** writing-paper
serie di pennarelli colorati	**5** set of coloured pens (*US* set of colored pens)
rotolo di carta da regalo	**6** roll of wrapping paper
fila di riviste	**7** row of magazines
pila di giornali	**8** pile of newspapers

At the Delicatessen page 27

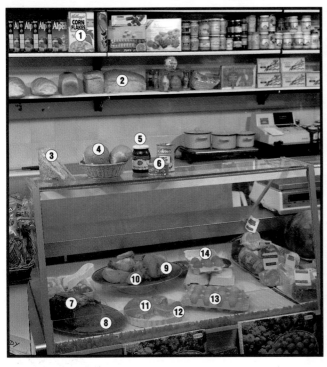

scatola di cereali	**1**	box of cereal
pagnotta	**2**	loaf of bread
tramezzini/sandwich	**3**	sandwiches
panino	**4**	roll
vasetto di marmellata	**5**	jar of jam/pot of jam
scatola di tonno	**6**	tin of tuna (*US* can of tuna)
pezzo di arrosto	**7**	joint of cooked meat (*US* roast)
fetta di carne	**8**	slice of meat
pollo arrosto	**9**	roast chicken
porzione di pollo	**10**	chicken portion (*US* piece of chicken)
torta salata	**11**	pie
fetta di torta salata	**12**	piece of pie
dozzina di uova	**13**	dozen eggs
mezza dozzina di uova	**14**	half a dozen eggs
biscotto	**15**	biscuit (*US* cookie)
pacco di biscotti	**16**	packet of biscuits (*US* package of cookies)
marmellata	**17**	jam
tonno	**18**	tuna

vasetto di yogurt	**19**	pot of yoghurt (*US* container of yogurt)
vaschetta di margarina	**20**	tub of margarine
cartone di succo d'arancia	**21**	carton of orange juice
formaggio	**22**	cheese
olive farcite	**23**	stuffed olives
pinta di latte	**24**	pint of milk
bottiglia di acqua minerale	**25**	bottle of mineral water
lattina di bibita gassata	**26**	can of fizzy drink (*US* can of soda)
yogurt	**27**	yoghurt (*esp US* yogurt)
margarina	**28**	margarine
burro	**29**	butter

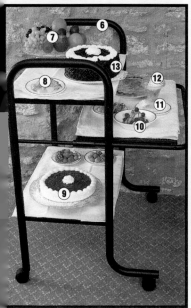

Antipasti	**Starters (*US* Appetizers)**		cameriere	**14** waiter
ciliegia	**1** cherry		menù	**15** menu
melone	**2** melon		Portate principali	**Main Courses**
salmone affumicato	**3** smoked salmon		rosbif	**16** roast beef
pâté con crostini	**4** pâté with toast		trota alle mandorle	**17** trout with almonds
zuppa di pomodoro	**5** tomato soup		bistecca	**18** steak
Dolci	**Desserts**		braciole di agnello	**19** lamb chops
carrello dei dolci	**6** dessert trolley		Contorni	**Vegetables**
	(*US* dessert cart)		granturco	**20** sweet corn (*US* corn)
frutta	**7** fruit		funghi	**21** mushrooms
torta di mele	**8** apple pie		insalata mista	**22** salad
torta al formaggio	**9** cheesecake		fagiolini	**23** runner beans
gelato con lamponi	**10** raspberry ice-cream			(*US* string beans)
macedonia di frutta	**11** fruit cocktail		piselli	**24** peas
panna	**12** cream		patata al forno	**25** jacket potato
torta al cioccolato	**13** chocolate gateau			(*esp US* baked potato)
	(*US* chocolate cake)		patate lesse	**26** boiled potatoes
			patate fritte	**27** chips (*US* French fries)

At the Camera Shop (*US* Camera Store)

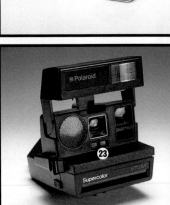

cliente	**1**	customer
ricevuta	**2**	receipt
registratore di cassa	**3**	cash register
treppiede	**4**	tripod
telescopio	**5**	telescope
commesso	**6**	shop assistant (*US* salesperson)
binocolo	**7**	binoculars
proiettore di diapositive	**8**	slide projector
diapositiva	**9**	slide
negativo	**10**	negative
rullino di pellicola	**11**	reel of film (*US* roll of film)
album per fotografie	**12**	photo album
stampa a colori	**13**	colour print (*US* color print)
stampa in bianco e nero	**14**	black and white print
zoom	**15**	zoom lens
macchina fotografica reflex	**16**	single lens reflex/SLR camera
obiettivo	**17**	lens
flash	**18**	flash (gun)
macchina compatta a 35 mm	**19**	35 mm* compact camer
flash incorporato	**20**	built-in flash
custodia per macchina fotografica	**21**	camera case
cinghia	**22**	strap
macchina fotografica Polaroid	**23**	polaroid camera
millimetro		**mm = millimetre (US millimeter)*

At the Hi-fi Shop (*US* Electronics Store)

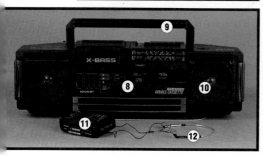

videocamera	**1**	camcorder
microfono	**2**	microphone
mirino	**3**	viewfinder
videocassetta	**4**	(video)tape
disco	**5**	record
cassetta	**6**	cassette
compact disc/CD	**7**	compact disc/CD
radioregistratore	**8**	radio cassette recorder (*US also* AM/FM cassette recorder)
manico	**9**	handle
altoparlante	**10**	speaker
Walkman	**11**	Walkman (*Brit also* personal stereo)
cuffie	**12**	headphones

impianto stereo	**13**	stereo/stereo system (*US also* sound system) (*Brit also* hi-fi)
giradischi	**14**	turntable
radio	**15**	radio
amplificatore	**16**	amplifier
equalizzatore grafico	**17**	graphic equalizer
piastra di registrazione	**18**	cassette deck/tape deck
lettore di compact disc	**19**	compact disc player/ CD player

Postal Services 1 page 31

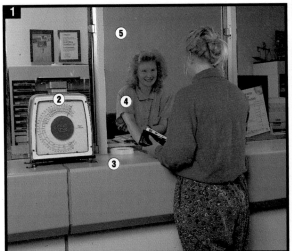

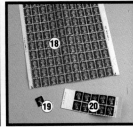

ufficio postale	**1**	post office
bilancia	**2**	scales (*US* scale)
bancone	**3**	counter
impiegata postale	**4**	counter assistant (*US* postal clerk)
sportello	**5**	window
levata	**6**	collection
furgone postale	**7**	post office van (*US* mail truck)
postino	**8**	postman (*US* mailman)
sacco postale	**9**	mailbag
posta	**10**	post (*US* mail)
buca delle lettere	**11**	letter-box/postbox (*US* mailbox)
distribuzione	**12**	delivery
borsa del postino	**13**	postbag (*esp US* mailbag)
cassetta delle lettere	**14**	letter-box (*US* mailbox)
recapito tramite corriere	**15**	delivery by courier (*US* delivery by messenger)
corriere	**16**	despatch-rider (*US* messenger)
distributore di francobolli	**17**	stamp machine
foglio di francobolli	**18**	sheet of stamps
francobollo	**19**	stamp
blocchetto di francobolli	**20**	book of stamps

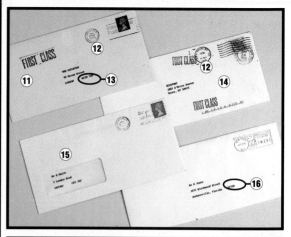

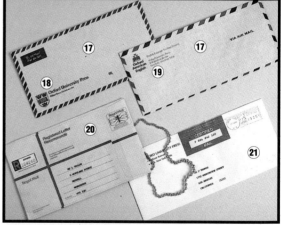

pacco postale	**1**	parcel (*esp US* package)
nastro da imballo	**2**	tape
etichetta	**3**	label
biglietto di auguri	**4**	greetings card (*US* greeting card)
lettera	**5**	letter
busta	**6**	envelope
linguetta/risvolto	**7**	flap
cartolina	**8**	postcard
messaggio	**9**	message
indirizzo	**10**	address
posta di prima classe	**11**	first-class post (*Brit*)
timbro postale	**12**	postmark
codice postale	**13**	postcode (*also* postal code) (*Brit*)
posta di prima classe	**14**	first class mail (*US*)
posta di seconda classe	**15**	second-class post (*Brit*)
codice postale	**16**	zip code (*US*)
posta aerea	**17**	airmail
indirizzo del mittente	**18**	address of sender (*Brit*)
indirizzo del mittente	**19**	return address (*US*)
posta raccomandata	**20**	registered post (*Brit*)
posta raccomandata	**21**	certified mail (*US*)
vaglia postale	**22**	postal order (*Brit*)
vaglia postale	**23**	money order (*US*)
lettera espresso	**24**	Special Delivery (*Brit*)
lettera espresso	**25**	Express Mail (*US*)

Numbers/The Date page 33

uno	**1** one
due	**2** two
tre	**3** three
quattro	**4** four
cinque	**5** five
sei	**6** six
sette	**7** seven
otto	**8** eight
nove	**9** nine
dieci	**10** ten
undici	**11** eleven
dodici	**12** twelve
tredici	**13** thirteen
quattordici	**14** fourteen
quindici	**15** fifteen
sedici	**16** sixteen
diciassette	**17** seventeen
diciotto	**18** eighteen
diciannove	**19** nineteen
venti	**20** twenty
ventuno	**21** twenty-one
trenta	**30** thirty
quaranta	**40** forty
cinquanta	**50** fifty
sessanta	**60** sixty
settanta	**70** seventy
ottanta	**80** eighty
novanta	**90** ninety
cento	**100** one hundred
centouno	**101** one hundred and one
mille	**1000** one thousand
duemiladuecentodieci	**2210** two thousand, two hundred and ten
un milione	**1000000** one million

JULY 1998

Sunday	5	12	19	26
Monday	6	13	20	27
Tuesday	7	14	21	28
Wednesday 1	8	15	22	29
Thursday 2	9	16	23	30
Friday 3	10	17	24	31
Saturday 4	11	18	25	

1° primo	**1st** first
2° secondo	**2nd** second
3° terzo	**3rd** third
4° quarto	**4th** fourth
5° quinto	**5th** fifth
6° sesto	**6th** sixth
7° settimo	**7th** seventh
8° ottavo	**8th** eighth
9° nono	**9th** ninth
10° decimo	**10th** tenth
11° undicesimo	**11th** eleventh
12° dodicesimo	**12th** twelfth
13° tredicesimo	**13th** thirteenth
20° ventesimo	**20th** twentieth
21° ventunesimo	**21st** twenty-first
22° ventiduesimo	**22nd** twenty-secon
23° ventitreesimo	**23rd** twenty-third
30° trentesimo	**30th** thirtieth
31° trentunesimo	**31st** thirty-first

Britannico **British**

3.5.98	3rd May 1998
3/5/98	3 May 1998

Il tre maggio	The third of May nineteen ninety-eight.
millenovecentonovantotto.	May the third, nineteen ninety-eight.

Americano **American**

Il tre maggio	5/3/98 May 3, 1998
millenovecentonovantotto.	May third, nineteen ninety-eight.

libretto degli assegni **1** cheque book
(*US* checkbook)

matrice **2** counterfoil/cheque stub
(*US* check stub)

carta assegni **3** cheque (guarantee) card
(*Brit only*)

carta di credito **4** credit card

estratto conto **5** bank statement
(*esp US* monthly statement)

saldo **6** (bank) balance

numero di conto corrente **7** (bank) account number

tassi di cambio **8** exchange rates

cassiere **9** cashier (*US* teller)

cambiare un traveller's cheque **10** changing a traveller's cheque (*US* cashing a traveler's check)

traveller's cheque **11** traveller's cheque
(*US* traveler's check)

cambiare valuta **12** changing money

valuta straniera **13** foreign currency

incassare un assegno **14** cashing a cheque
(*US* cashing a check)

prelevare denaro contante **15** withdrawing cash

cassa automatica **16** cash dispenser/cashpoint
(*US* cash machine/
automatic teller)

fare un versamento **17** paying in
(*US* making a deposit)

ricevuta di versamento **18** paying-in slip
(*US* deposit slip)

ricevuta di prelievo **19** withdrawal slip

American Money

1¢/$0.01	5¢/$0.05	10¢/$0.10	25¢/$0.25

monete	**1 coins**	
una moneta da un centesimo	**2** a penny	
una moneta da cinque centesimi	**3** a nickel	
una moneta da dieci centesimi	**4** a dime	
una moneta da venticinque centesimi	**5** a quarter	

banconote	**6 bills**	
una banconota da un dollaro	**7** a dollar bill	$1
una banconota da cinque dollari	**8** a five dollar bill	$5
una banconota da dieci dollari	**9** a ten dollar bill	$10
una banconota da venti dollari	**10** a twenty dollar bill	$20
una banconota da cinquanta dollari	**11** a fifty dollar bill	$50

Pagamento in contanti	**Paying (in) cash**
venti dollari	**12** twenty dollars
sette dollari e novantacinque centesimi/ sette e novantacinque	**13** seven dollars and ninety-five cents/ seven ninety-five
scontrino	**14** receipt
totale	**15** total
resto	**16** change

British Money

②	③	④	⑤	⑥	⑦	⑧	⑨
1p/£0.01	2p/£0.02	5p/£0.05	10p/£0.10	20p/£0.20	50p/£0.50	£1	£2

	monete	**1 coins**
una moneta da un penny	**2**	a one pence piece/a penny
una moneta da due penny	**3**	a two pence piece
una moneta da cinque penny	**4**	a five pence piece
una moneta da dieci penny	**5**	a ten pence piece
una moneta da venti penny	**6**	a twenty pence piece
una moneta da cinquanta penny	**7**	a fifty pence piece
una moneta da una sterlina	**8**	a pound coin
una moneta da due sterline	**9**	a two pound coin

	banconote	**10 notes**
banconota da cinque sterline	**11**	a five pound note
banconota da dieci sterline	**12**	a ten pound note
banconota da venti sterline	**13**	a twenty pound note
banconota da cinquanta sterline	**14**	a fifty pound note

Quanto costa?	**How much is it?**
venti penny	**15** twenty pence (*also* 20p)
dieci penny	**16** ten pence (*also* 10p)
cinquanta penny	**17** fifty pence (*also* 50p)
tre sterline e	**18** three pounds
ottantadue penny/	eighty-two pence/
tre sterline ottantadue	three pounds eighty-two
due sterline	**19** two pounds

Time

24 hours = 1 day
7 days = 1 week (wk)
365 days = 1 year (yr)
100 years = 1 century (c)

le tre **1** three o'clock

quadrante **2** clock-face

lancetta dei minuti **3** minute-hand

lancetta delle ore **4** hour-hand

lancetta dei secondi **5** second-hand

le nove e cinque **6** five past nine
(*US also* five after nine)/
nine o five

le nove e dieci **7** ten past nine
(*US also* ten after nine)/
nine ten

le nove e un quarto **8** a quarter past nine
(*US also* a quarter after nine)/
nine fifteen

le nove e mezzo/trenta **9** half past nine/nine thirty

le dieci meno venti/le nove **10** twenty to ten/nine forty
e quaranta

un quarto alle dieci/ **11** a quarter to ten/
le nove e quarantacinque nine forty-five

dieci alle dieci/le nove **12** ten to ten/nine fifty
e cinquanta

le dodici/mezzogiorno/ **13** twelve o'clock/midday
mezzanotte (*esp US* noon) *also* midnight

le dodici e sette **14** seven minutes past twelve
(*US also* seven minutes
after twelve)/twelve o seven

le sette/ **15** seven am (*US* A.M.)/
le sette di mattina seven o'clock in the morning

le diciassette/ **16** five pm (*US* P.M.)/
le cinque di pomeriggio five o'clock in the afternoon

le venti/ **17** eight pm (*US* P.M.)/
le otto di sera eight o'clock in the evening

le ventitré e trenta/ **18** eleven thirty pm (*US* P.M.)/
le undici e mezzo di notte half past eleven at night

07:00

17:00

20:00

23:30

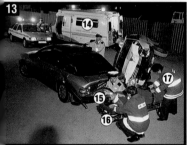

Polizia	**Police**
commissariato	**1** police station
automobile della polizia	**2** police car
poliziotto	**3** police officer
Vigili del fuoco	**Fire Brigade**
	(*US* Fire Department)
autopompa	**4** fire-engine
scala	**5** ladder
acqua	**6** water
fumo	**7** smoke
fuoco/incendio	**8** fire
estintore	**9** fire extinguisher
pompiere	**10** fireman
	(*esp US* fire fighter)
idrante	**11** hydrant
tubo flessibile	**12** hose
Servizio di ambulanza	**Ambulance Service**
incidente stradale	**13** car accident
ambulanza	**14** ambulance
ferito	**15** injured man
barella/lettiga	**16** stretcher
personale paramedico	**17** paramedic
prefisso internazionale	**18** international code
prefisso internazionale	**19** country code
prefisso della città	**20** area code
numero di telefono	**21** (tele)phone number
cabina telefonica	**22** (tele)phone box
	(*esp US* telephone booth)
ricevitore	**23** receiver
scheda telefonica	**24** phonecard (*Brit only*)
fessura per la moneta	**25** slot
composizione del numero di telefono	**26** dial

⑱ ⑲
00 44 1865 556767
01865 556767
⑳ ㉑

Britain the telephone number for the
olice, fire and ambulance services is 999.
the US the emergency number is 911.

Gran Bretagna il numero di telefono
er polizia, vigili del fuoco e ambulanza è
99. Negli Stati Uniti il numero per i
rvizi di emergenza è 911.

Jobs 1 page 39

artista	**1** artist
giardiniere	**2** gardener
disc jockey	**3** disc jockey (*US* disk jockey)
presentatrice del telegiornale	**4** newsreader (*esp US* newscaster)

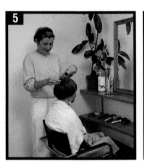   

parrucchiera	**5** hairdresser
farmacista	**6** pharmacist
fornaio/panettiere	**7** baker
macellaio	**8** butcher

agricoltore	**9** farmer
pescatore	**10** fisherman
marinaio	**11** sailor
soldato	**12** soldier

   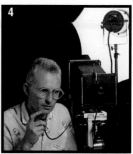

architetto	**1**	architect
camionista	**2**	lorry driver (*US* truck driver)
agente di viaggi	**3**	travel agent
fotografo	**4**	photographer

 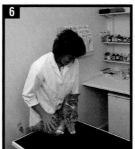  

programmatore di computer	**5**	computer programmer
veterinario	**6**	vet
elettricista	**7**	electrician
falegname	**8**	carpenter

saldatore	**9**	welder
idraulico	**10**	plumber
meccanico	**11**	mechanic
muratore	**12**	bricklayer

Daily Routine   page 41

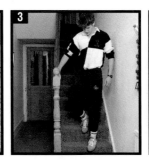

Si sveglia.	**1** He wakes up.
Si alza.	**2** He gets up/He gets out of bed.
Scende le scale.	**3** He goes downstairs.
Va a correre.	**4** He goes jogging.

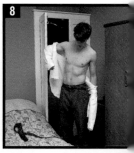

Torna a casa.	**5** He comes back.
Prende la posta.	**6** He picks up the post (*US* mail).
Si fa la doccia.	**7** He has a shower.
	(*esp US* He takes a shower.)
Si veste.	**8** He gets dressed.

Fa colazione.	**9** He has breakfast/He eats breakfast
Esce di casa.	**10** He leaves home.
Compra il giornale.	**11** He buys a newspaper.
Ascolta della musica.	**12** He listens to music.

Prende il treno.	**13** He catches the train.
Legge il giornale.	**14** He reads the newspaper.
Comincia a lavorare.	**15** He starts work.
Prende un caffè.	**16** He has a cup of coffee.
Beve un caffè.	He drinks some coffee.

Pranza.	**17** He has lunch/He eats lunch.
Finisce di lavorare.	**18** He finishes work.
Va in macchina al centro sportivo.	**19** He drives to the sports centre (*US* health club).
Incontra gli amici.	**20** He meets his friends.

Gioca a squash.	**21** He plays squash.
Cena.	**22** He has dinner/He eats dinner.
Guarda la televisione.	**23** He watches television/TV.
Va a letto.	**24** He goes to bed.

Office Verbs page 43

  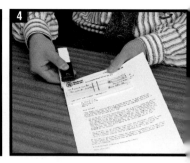

Sta dettando una lettera.	**1** She is dictating a letter.
dittafono	**2** Dictaphone/dictating machine
Sta battendo a macchina una lettera.	**3** He is typing a letter.
Sta battendo a macchina.	He is typing.
Sta attaccando un assegno ad una lettera con la cucitrice.	**4** He is stapling a cheque to a letter. (*US* check)

Sta compilando un modulo.	**5** She is filling in a form.
	(*US* She is filling out a form.)
Sta firmando una lettera.	**6** She is signing a letter.
firma	**7** signature
Sta prendendo nota di un appuntamento.	**8** She is making a note of an appointment.

  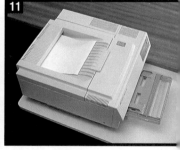

Sta archiviando una pratica.	**9** He is filing.
Sta mandando un fax.	**10** He is sending a fax.
Sta mandando una lettera per fax.	He is faxing a letter.
Sta stampando.	**11** It is printing.
Sta stampando una copia.	It is printing a copy.

bacheca	**1** notice-board	pratica	**14** file
	(*US* bulletin board)	schedario	**15** filing cabinet
calendario	**2** calendar		(*US* file cabinet)
posta in arrivo	**3** in-tray (*US* in box)	raccoglitore ad anelli	**16** ring binder
posta in partenza	**4** out-tray (*US* out box)	tende alla veneziana	**17** venetian blind
segreteria telefonica	**5** answering machine	stampato/tabulato	**18** printout
	(*Brit also* answerphone)	stampante	**19** printer
scrivania	**6** desk	segretario	**20** secretary
perforatrice	**7** hole-punch	agenda	**21** diary
schedario	**8** card index (*US* card file)		(*US* appointment book)
cancellino	**9** Tipp-Ex	tastiera	**22** keyboard
	(*esp US* correction fluid)	dischetto	**23** floppy disk
graffetta	**10** paper-clip	disk drive	**24** disk drive
chiave	**11** key	personal computer	**25** personal computer/PC
cucitrice	**12** stapler	schermo	**26** screen
bloc-notes/blocco per appunti	**13** notebook	macchina da scrivere	**27** typewriter

A Science Laboratory 1

occhiali di protezione	**1** goggles		siringa	**16** syringe
provetta	**2** test-tube		beuta conica	**17** conical flask
fiamma	**3** flame		tubo a U	**18** U-tube
tubo di gomma	**4** rubber tubing		sgabello	**19** stool
becco Bunsen	**5** Bunsen burner		sostegno a morsetto	**20** clamp stand
rastrelliera	**6** rack			(*US* ring stand)
pestello	**7** pestle		termometro	**21** thermometer
mortaio	**8** mortar		beuta a fondo circolare	**22** round bottom flask
beuta a fondo piatto	**9** flat bottom flask		condensatore	**23** condenser
imbuto	**10** funnel		bicchiere graduato	**24** measuring beaker
carta filtrante	**11** filter paper			(*US* graduated beaker)
prisma	**12** prism		reticella metallica	**25** gauze
molle	**13** tongs			(*US* wire mesh screen)
lente di ingrandimento	**14** magnifying glass		treppiede	**26** tripod
stantuffo	**15** plunger			

camice da laboratorio	**1** lab coat	pila/batteria	**14** battery
asticella di vetro	**2** glass rod	carrello	**15** trolley (*US* cart)
cilindro graduato	**3** measuring cylinder	cronometro	**16** stop clock (*US* timer)
	(*US* graduated cylinder)	microscopio	**17** microscope
tappo	**4** stopper	regolatore della messa a fuoco	**18** focusing control
filo conduttore	**5** wire		(*US also* focusing knob)
elettrodo	**6** electrode	piatto portaoggetti	**19** stage
morsetto	**7** crocodile clip	vetrino	**20** slide
	(*US* alligator clip)	obiettivo	**21** objective lens
calamita	**8** magnet	oculare	**22** eyepiece
capsula di Petri	**9** Petri dish (*US* petri dish)	bilancia	**23** balance/scales (*US* scale)
spatola	**10** spatula	bilancia a molla	**24** spring balance
contagocce	**11** dropper	buretta	**25** burette
pipetta	**12** pipette	crogiolo	**26** crucible
peso	**13** weight	microbilancia	**27** microbalance

Shapes and Lines page 47

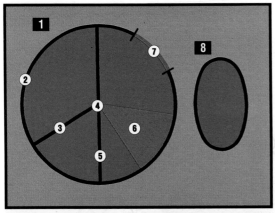

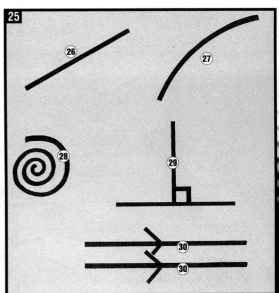

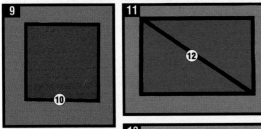

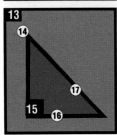

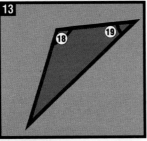

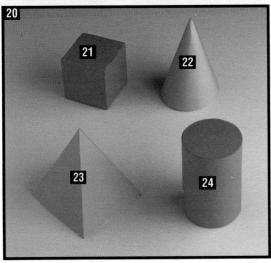

cerchio	**1**	circle
circonferenza	**2**	circumference
raggio	**3**	radius
centro	**4**	centre (*US* center)
diametro	**5**	diameter
settore circolare	**6**	sector
arco	**7**	arc
ovale	**8**	oval
quadrato	**9**	square
lato	**10**	side
rettangolo	**11**	rectangle
diagonale	**12**	diagonal
triangolo	**13**	triangle
vertice	**14**	apex
angolo retto	**15**	right angle
base	**16**	base
ipotenusa	**17**	hypotenuse
angolo ottuso	**18**	obtuse angle
angolo acuto	**19**	acute angle
figure solide	**20**	solid figures
cubo	**21**	cube
cono	**22**	cone
piramide	**23**	pyramid
cilindro	**24**	cylinder
linee	**25**	lines
linea retta	**26**	straight line
linea curva	**27**	curve
spirale	**28**	spiral
retta perpendicolare	**29**	perpendicular li
rette parallele	**30**	parallel lines

$$7 \overset{⑪}{+} 11 = 18$$

$$80 \overset{⑫}{-} 13 = 67$$

$$40 \overset{⑬}{\times} 4 = 160$$

$$32 \div 8 \overset{⑭}{} \overset{⑮}{=} 4$$

$$\overset{⑯}{2.5} \qquad \overset{⑰}{50\%}$$

profondità	**1**	depth
altezza	**2**	height
larghezza	**3**	width
spigolo	**4**	edge
angolo	**5**	corner
lunghezza	**6**	length
parte anteriore	**7**	front
fondo	**8**	bottom
lato	**9**	side
retro	**10**	back
più	**11**	plus
meno	**12**	minus
per	**13**	multiplied by/times
diviso	**14**	divided by
uguale	**15**	equals
due virgola cinque	**16**	two point five
cinquanta per cento	**17**	fifty per cent
frazioni	**18**	fractions
un quarto	**19**	a quarter/ ¼
un terzo	**20**	a third/ ⅓
la metà	**21**	a half/ ½
tre quarti	**22**	three quarters/ ¾
peso	**23**	weight
10 grammi	**24**	10 grams*
chilogrammo	**25**	kilogram*
capacità	**26**	capacity
millilitro	**27**	millilitre (*US* milliliter)*
litro	**28**	litre (*US* liter)*
millimetro	**29**	millimetre (*US* millimeter)*
centimetro	**30**	centimetre (*US* centimeter)*

Queste unità di misura non sono solitamente usate nell'inglese americano.

*These measurements are not usually used in US English.

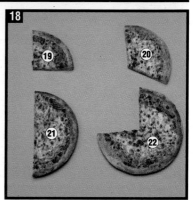

1000 grams (g) = 1 kilogram (kg)

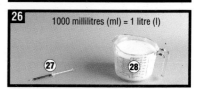

1000 millilitres (ml) = 1 litre (l)

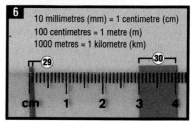

10 millimetres (mm) = 1 centimetre (cm)
100 centimetres = 1 metre (m)
1000 metres = 1 kilometre (km)

cm   1   2   3   4

The Classroom

lavagna	**1**	blackboard (*US also* chalkboard)
alunna	**2**	pupil (*esp US* student)
libro di testo	**3**	textbook
quaderno	**4**	exercise book (*US* notebook)
calcolatrice	**5**	calculator
squadra	**6**	set square (*US* triangle)
goniometro	**7**	protractor
cartella	**8**	school bag
pavimento	**9**	(tiled) floor
sedia	**10**	chair
mappamondo	**11**	globe
forbici	**12**	scissors
cavalletto	**13**	easel
pennello	**14**	paintbrush
scatola di colori	**15**	paintbox
insegnante	**16**	teacher
disegno	**17**	picture
carta geografica	**18**	map

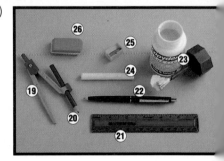

compasso	**19**	(pair of) compasses (*also* compass)
matita	**20**	pencil
righello	**21**	ruler
penna	**22**	pen
colla	**23**	glue
gesso	**24**	(piece of) chalk
temperamatite	**25**	pencil-sharpener
gomma da cancellare	**26**	rubber (*US* eraser)

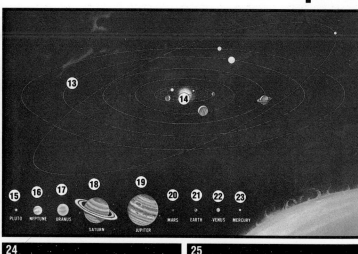

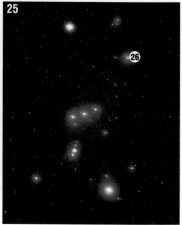

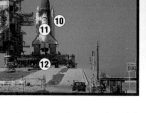

luna nuova/crescente	**1** new moon
	(*esp US* crescent moon)
mezza luna	**2** half moon
	(*US also* first quarter)
luna piena	**3** full moon
luna calante	**4** old moon
	(*US* half moon/last quarter)
modulo lunare	**5** lunar module
astronauta	**6** astronaut
tuta spaziale	**7** spacesuit
veicolo lunare	**8** lunar vehicle
satellite	**9** satellite
razzo	**10** rocket
navetta spaziale	**11** space shuttle
piattaforma di lancio	**12** launch pad

Il sistema solare	**The Solar System**
orbita	**13** orbit
Sole	**14** Sun
I pianeti	**The Planets**
Plutone	**15** Pluto
Nettuno	**16** Neptune
Urano	**17** Uranus
Saturno	**18** Saturn
Giove	**19** Jupiter
Marte	**20** Mars
Terra	**21** Earth
Venere	**22** Venus
Mercurio	**23** Mercury
Spazio interstellare	**Outer Space**
galassia	**24** galaxy
costellazione	**25** constellation
stella	**26** star

The Weather page 51

C'è sole.	**1**	It's sunny.
Piove.	**2**	It's raining. (*US also* It's rainy.)
Nevica.	**3**	It's snowing. (*US also* It's snowy.)
neve	**4**	snow
C'è vento.	**5**	It's windy.

C'è foschia.	**6**	It's misty.
C'è nebbia.	**7**	It's foggy.
È nuvoloso.	**8**	It's cloudy.
Minaccia tempesta.	**9**	It's stormy.

temporale	**10**	thunderstorm
lampo/fulmine	**11**	lightning
arcobaleno	**12**	rainbow
È sereno.	**13**	It's bright.
È coperto.	**14**	It's dull. (*US* It's dark.)

The Temperature
The Seasons

SHORT & MASON
LONDON

F | C
120 — 50 ①②
110 — 40
100 —
90 — 30 ③
80 — ④
70 — 20 ⑤
60 —
50 — 10 ⑥
40 — 0 ⑦
30 —
20 — ⑧

MADE IN ENGLAND

Le stagioni The Seasons

in primavera **9** in (the) spring
in estate **10** in (the) summer
in autunno **11** in (the) autumn
(*US* in the fall)
in inverno **12** in (the) winter

I mesi The Months

gennaio January
febbraio February
marzo March
aprile April
maggio May
giugno June
luglio July
agosto August
settembre September
ottobre October
novembre November
dicembre December

La temperatura The Temperature

gradi Fahrenheit **1** degrees Fahrenheit
gradi centigradi **2** degrees Celsius
(*or* centigrade)
Fa molto caldo. **3** It's hot.
Fa caldo. **4** It's warm.
Fa fresco. **5** It's cool.
Fa freddo. **6** It's cold.
Fa molto freddo. **7** It's freezing.
Fa sei gradi sotto zero. **8** It's minus six (degrees).
(*US* It's six (degrees)
below zero.)

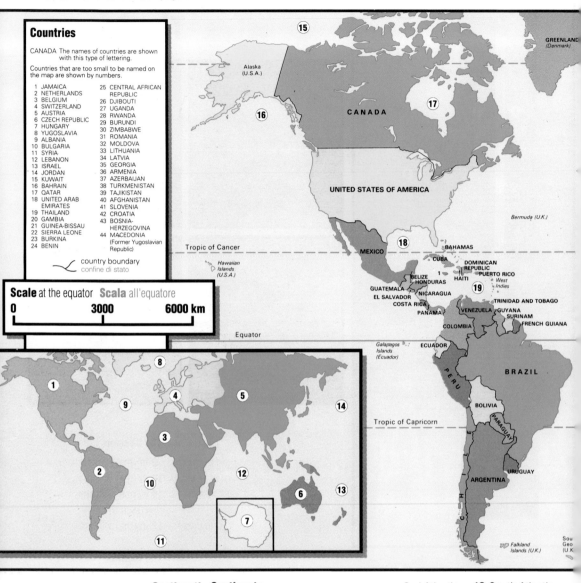

Countries

CANADA The names of countries are shown with this type of lettering.

Countries that are too small to be named on the map are shown by numbers.

1	JAMAICA	25	CENTRAL AFRICAN REPUBLIC
2	NETHERLANDS	26	DJIBOUTI
3	BELGIUM	27	UGANDA
4	SWITZERLAND	28	RWANDA
5	AUSTRIA	29	BURUNDI
6	CZECH REPUBLIC	30	ZIMBABWE
7	HUNGARY	31	ROMANIA
8	YUGOSLAVIA	32	MOLDOVA
9	ALBANIA	33	LITHUANIA
10	BULGARIA	34	LATVIA
11	SYRIA	35	GEORGIA
12	LEBANON	36	ARMENIA
13	ISRAEL	37	AZERBAIJAN
14	JORDAN	38	TURKMENISTAN
15	KUWAIT	39	TAJIKISTAN
16	BAHRAIN	40	AFGHANISTAN
17	QATAR	41	SLOVENIA
18	UNITED ARAB EMIRATES	42	CROATIA
19	THAILAND	43	BOSNIA-HERZEGOVINA
20	GAMBIA	44	MACEDONIA (Former Yugoslavian Republic)
21	GUINEA-BISSAU		
22	SIERRA LEONE		
23	BURKINA		
24	BENIN		

country boundary
confine di stato

Scale at the equator Scala all'equatore

0   3000   6000 km

Continenti	Continents		Sud Atlantico	10 South Atlantic
Nord America	**1** North America		Oceano Antartico	**11** Antarctic
Sud America	**2** South America		Oceano Indiano	**12** Indian
Africa	**3** Africa		Sud Pacifico	**13** South Pacific
Europa	**4** Europe		Nord Pacifico	**14** North Pacific
Asia	**5** Asia		**Mari, golfi, e baie**	**Seas, Gulfs, and Bay**
Australia	**6** Australia		Mare di Beaufort	**15** Beaufort Sea
Antartide	**7** Antarctica		Golfo dell'Alaska	**16** Gulf of Alaska
Oceani	**Oceans**		Baia di Hudson	**17** Hudson Bay
Oceano Artico	**8** Arctic		Golfo del Messico	**18** Gulf of Mexico
Nord Atlantico	**9** North Atlantic		Mar dei Caraibi	**19** Caribbean Sea

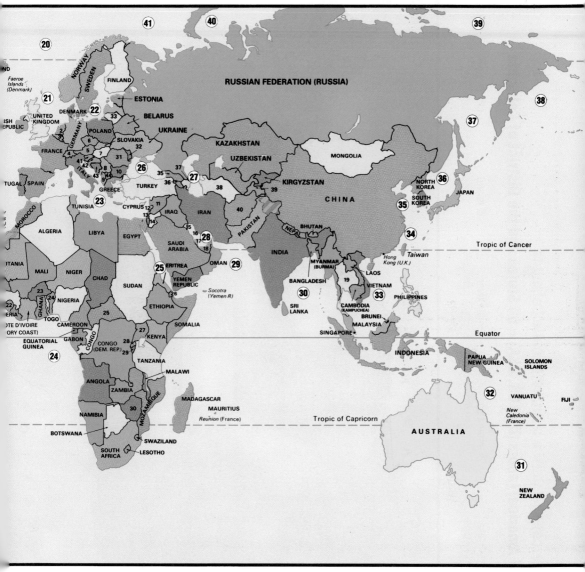

Mar di Norvegia	**20** Norwegian Sea		Mare di Tasman	**31** Tasman Sea
Mare del Nord	**21** North Sea		Mar dei Coralli	**32** Coral Sea
Mar Baltico	**22** Baltic Sea		Mar Cinese Meridionale	**33** South China Sea
Mare Mediterraneo	**23** Mediterranean Sea		Mar Cinese Orientale	**34** East China Sea
Golfo di Guinea	**24** Gulf of Guinea		Mar Giallo	**35** Yellow Sea
Mar Rosso	**25** Red Sea		Mare del Giappone	**36** Sea of Japan
Mar Nero	**26** Black Sea		Mare di Okhotsk	**37** Sea of Okhotsk
Mar Caspio	**27** Caspian Sea		Mare di Bering	**38** Bering Sea
Golfo Persico	**28** The Gulf		Mare di Laptev	**39** Laptev Sea
Mare Arabico	**29** Arabian Sea		Mare di Kara	**40** Kara Sea
Golfo del Bengala	**30** Bay of Bengal		Mare di Barents	**41** Barents Sea

The USA

page 55

gli Stati Uniti (d'America) = 50 Stati e il Distretto della Columbia

the United States (of America) (*abbrs* (the) US, USA) = 50 States and the District of Columbia

Legend:
- ----- state line / confine di stato
- mountain / regione montuosa
- lake / lago
- main river / fiume principale
- island / isola
- city *or* town / città

Scale
0   500 km

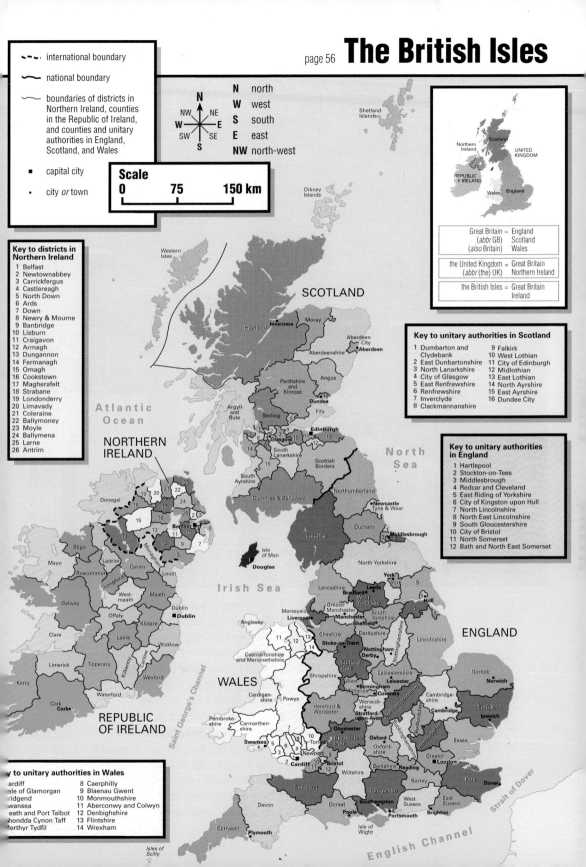

--- international boundary

--- national boundary

--- boundaries of districts in Northern Ireland, counties in the Republic of Ireland, and counties and unitary authorities in England, Scotland, and Wales

■ capital city

• city or town

N north
W west
S south
E east
NW north-west

Scale

0   75   150 km

Great Britain = England
(abbr GB)   Scotland
(also Britain)   Wales

the United Kingdom = Great Britain
(abbr (the) UK)   Northern Ireland

the British Isles = Great Britain
Ireland

Key to districts in Northern Ireland

1 Belfast
2 Newtownabbey
3 Carrickfergus
4 Castlereagh
5 North Down
6 Ards
7 Down
8 Newry & Mourne
9 Banbridge
10 Lisburn
11 Craigavon
12 Armagh
13 Dungannon
14 Fermanagh
15 Omagh
16 Cookstown
17 Magherafelt
18 Strabane
19 Londonderry
20 Limavady
21 Coleraine
22 Ballymoney
23 Moyle
24 Ballymena
25 Larne
26 Antrim

Key to unitary authorities in Scotland

1 Dumbarton and Clydebank
2 East Dunbartonshire
3 North Lanarkshire
4 City of Glasgow
5 East Renfrewshire
6 Renfrewshire
7 Inverclyde
8 Clackmannanshire
9 Falkirk
10 West Lothian
11 City of Edinburgh
12 Midlothian
13 East Lothian
14 North Ayrshire
15 East Ayrshire
16 Dundee City

Key to unitary authorities in England

1 Hartlepool
2 Stockton-on-Tees
3 Middlesbrough
4 Redcar and Cleveland
5 East Riding of Yorkshire
6 City of Kingston upon Hull
7 North Lincolnshire
8 North East Lincolnshire
9 South Gloucestershire
10 City of Bristol
11 North Somerset
12 Bath and North East Somerset

Key to unitary authorities in Wales

Cardiff   8 Caerphilly
Vale of Glamorgan   9 Blaenau Gwent
Bridgend   10 Monmouthshire
Swansea   11 Aberconwy and Colwyn
Neath and Port Talbot   12 Denbighshire
Rhondda Cynon Taff   13 Flintshire
Merthyr Tydfil   14 Wrexham

Shetland Islands

Orkney Islands

SCOTLAND

Western Isles

Highland

Inverness

Moray

Aberdeenshire

Aberdeen City
Aberdeen

Perthshire and Kinross

Angus

Dundee

Fife

Argyll and Bute

Stirling

Edinburgh

Glasgow

South Lanarkshire

Scottish Borders

South Ayrshire

Dumfries & Galloway

Northumberland

Newcastle Tyne & Wear

Durham

Cumbria

Middlesbrough

Atlantic Ocean

NORTHERN IRELAND

Donegal

Belfast

North Sea

ENGLAND

Sligo

Mayo

Leitrim

Roscommon

Longford

Cavan

Westmeath

Meath

Louth

Galway

Offaly

Dublin

Clare

Laois

Kildare

Wicklow

Limerick

Tipperary

Kilkenny

Carlow

Wexford

Kerry

Waterford

Cork

REPUBLIC OF IRELAND

Isle of Man

Douglas

Irish Sea

North Yorkshire

York

Lancashire

Bradford

Leeds

West Yorkshire

South Yorkshire

Hull

Greater Manchester

Liverpool

Manchester

Merseyside

Anglesey

Sheffield

Cheshire

Derbyshire

Stoke-on-Trent

Staffordshire

Nottingham

Derby

Nottinghamshire

Lincolnshire

Caernarfonshire and Merionethshire

WALES

Shropshire

West Midlands

Birmingham

Leicestershire

Leicester

Cardiganshire

Powys

Hereford & Worcester

Coventry

Warwickshire

Stratford-upon-Avon

Cambridgeshire

Cambridge

Norfolk

Norwich

Suffolk

Ipswich

Pembrokeshire

Carmarthenshire

Gloucester

Gloucestershire

Oxford

Oxfordshire

Buckinghamshire

Bedfordshire

Northamptonshire

Hertfordshire

Essex

Greater London

Swansea

Newport

Cardiff

Bristol

Wiltshire

Berkshire

Reading

Surrey

Kent

Dover

Devon

Somerset

Hampshire

West Sussex

East Sussex

Brighton

Dorset

Poole

Portsmouth

Southampton

Isle of Wight

Cornwall

Plymouth

Saint George's Channel

Strait of Dover

English Channel

Isles of Scilly

Prepositions 1 page 57

Sta guardando fuori dalla finestra.	**1** She is looking **out of** the window.
Sta attraversando il cortile.	**2** She is walking **across** the courtyard.
L'albero sta crescendo attraverso la panca.	**3** The tree is growing **through** the seat.
Sta gettando della carta nel cestino.	**4** He is throwing some paper **into** the bin (*US* trash can).
Sta gettando della carta per terra.	**5** He is throwing some paper **onto** the ground.
Sta andando in biblioteca.	**6** She is going **to** the library.
Sta venendo dalla biblioteca.	**7** He is coming **from** the library.
La carta sta cadendo dal tavolo.	**8** The paper is falling **off** the table.
Si sta allontanando dalla bacheca.	**9** She is walking **away from** the notice (*US* sign).
Si sta dirigendo verso la bacheca.	**10** She is walking **towards** (*esp US* **toward**) the notice (*US* sig
Sta salendo le scale.	**11** She is walking **up** the steps.
I fiori crescono lungo il muro.	**12** The flowers are growing **along** the wall.
Sta scendendo le scale.	**13** He is walking **down** the steps.
Sta guardando oltre il balcone.	**14** He is looking **over** the balcony.

Il cespuglio è fuori dalla finestra.	**1** The bush is **outside** the window.
Il nastro è attorno al cesto.	**2** The ribbon is **round** the basket (*esp US* **around** the basket).
Le cassette sono nel cassetto.	**3** The cassettes are **in/inside** the drawer.
Il libro è appoggiato al il tavolino.	**4** The book is **against** the table.
La tazza è sotto il tavolino.	**5** The mug is **under/underneath** the table.
Il tavolino è vicino al caminetto.	**6** The table is **by/near** the fireplace.
I fiori secchi sono nel caminetto.	**7** The dried flowers are **in** the fireplace.
L'orologio è tra le candele.	**8** The clock is **between** the candles.
La candela è sulla mensola del camino.	**9** The candle is **on** the mantelpiece (*US* mantel).
Il quadro è sopra la mensola del camino.	**10** The picture is **over** the mantelpiece (*US* mantel).
La pianta è sopra la libreria.	**11** The plant is **on top of** the bookcase.
Il soprammobile è nella parte superiore della libreria.	**12** The ornament is **at the top of** the bookcase.
Il piatto è nel centro della libreria.	**13** The plate is **in the middle of** the bookcase.
I libri sono alla base della libreria.	**14** The books are **at the bottom of** the bookcase.
I piatti sono sopra i libri.	**15** The plates are **above** the books.
Le tazze sono sotto la teiera.	**16** The cups are **below** the teapot.
La teiera è vicina al piatto.	**17** The teapot is **beside/next to** the plate.
La televisione è davanti alle riviste.	**18** The television is **in front of** the magazines.
Le riviste sono dietro alla televisione.	**19** The magazines are **behind** the television.

segnale stradale	**1**	road sign
avviso di parcheggio	**2**	parking notice (*US* parking sign)
buca delle lettere	**3**	letter-box/pillar-box (*US* mailbox)
bar	**4**	café (*also* cafe)
poliziotto	**5**	police officer
marciapiede	**6**	pavement (*US* sidewalk)
tombino	**7**	manhole cover
canale di scolo	**8**	gutter
bordo del marciapiede	**9**	kerb (*US* curb)
strada	**10**	street
angolo della strada	**11**	street corner
negozio	**12**	shop (*esp US* store)
traffico	**13**	traffic
cestino per rifiuti	**14**	litter-bin (*US* trash can/garbage can)
edicola	**15**	news-stand
giornale	**16**	newspaper
venditore di giornali	**17**	news-vendor (*Brit only*)
grande magazzino	**18**	department store
bandiera	**19**	flag
cartellone pubblicitario	**20**	advertisement
pensilina	**21**	bus shelter
fermata dell'autobus	**22**	bus stop
fabbrica	**23**	factory
passaggio pedonale	**24**	pedestrian crossing (*US* crosswalk)

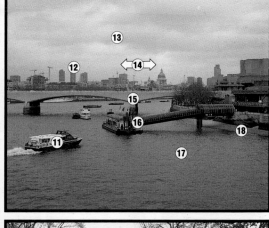

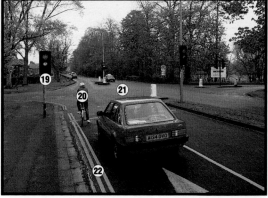

edificio	**1** building
parco	**2** park
carrozzina	**3** pram (*US* baby carriage)
passeggino	**4** pushchair (*US* stroller)
traversa	**5** side street
taxi	**6** taxi/cab
lampione	**7** lamppost
pedone	**8** pedestrian
ringhiera	**9** railings
insegna stradale	**10** street sign
imbarcazione	**11** boat
grattacielo	**12** tower block
	(*esp US* skyscraper)
cielo	**13** sky
orizzonte	**14** skyline
ponte	**15** bridge
pontile	**16** pier
fiume	**17** river
riva/sponda	**18** bank
In periferia	**In the suburbs**
semaforo	**19** traffic-lights
	(*US* traffic light)
ciclista	**20** cyclist (*US* bicyclist)
incrocio	**21** crossroads
	(*US* intersection)
doppia linea gialla	**22** double yellow lines
	(*Brit only*)

indicazione stradale	**23** signpost
macchina/automobile	**24** car
autobus a due piani	**25** double-decker bus
rotatoria	**26** roundabout
	(*US* traffic circle/rotary)

Roads and Road Signs 1 page 61

dare la precedenza	**1**	give way (*US* yield)
arresto all'incrocio	**2**	stop
divieto di accesso	**3**	no entry (*US* do not enter)
doppio senso di circolazione	**4**	two-way traffic
divieto di inversione ad U	**5**	no U-turn
limite di velocità	**6**	speed limit
divieto di svolta a sinistra	**7**	no left turn
doppia curva, la prima a destra	**8**	bend to right (*US* curve to right)
pista ciclabile e viale pedonale	**9**	cycle and pedestrian route (*US* bike and pedestrian pat...
strada a senso unico	**10**	one-way street
area di servizio	**11**	service station (*US* service area)
svolta a destra obbligatoria	**12**	turn right
lavori stradali	**13**	roadworks (*US* road work)
autocarro con cassone ribaltabile	**14**	dumper (truck) (*esp US* dump truck)
addetto ai lavori stradali	**15**	construction worker
martello pneumatico	**16**	pneumatic drill (*US also* jackhammer)
cono	**17**	cone
ruspa	**18**	JCB (*US* backhoe)
terra	**19**	soil

autostrada	**1**	motorway (*Brit*)
raccordo di entrata	**2**	slip-road (*Brit*)
banchina/terrapieno	**3**	embankment (*Brit*)
corsia per soste di emergenza	**4**	hard shoulder (*Brit*)
corsia per veicoli lenti	**5**	inside lane/slow lane (*Brit*)
corsia centrale	**6**	middle lane/centre lane (*Brit*)
corsia di sorpasso	**7**	outside lane/fast lane (*Brit*)
banchina spartitraffico	**8**	central reservation (*Brit*)
guardrail centrale	**9**	crash barrier (*Brit*)
cavalcavia	**10**	flyover (*Brit*)
autostrada	**11**	freeway/ interstate highway (*US*)
raccordo di uscita	**12**	exit ramp (*US*)
banchina/terrapieno	**13**	bank (*US*)
corsia per soste di emergenza	**14**	shoulder (*US*)
corsia per veicoli lenti	**15**	right lane/slow lane (*US*)
corsia centrale	**16**	center lane/middle lane (*US*)
corsia di sorpasso	**17**	left lane/fast lane/ passing lane (*US*)
banchina spartitraffico	**18**	median strip (*US*)
guardrail centrale	**19**	guardrail (*US*)
cavalcavia	**20**	overpass (*US*)

sottopassaggio	**21**	underpass
ponte pedonale	**22**	footbridge
ciglio erboso	**23**	grass verge (*US* shoulder)
strada	**24**	road (*US* highway)
nodo stradale	**25**	junction (*esp US* intersection)

Vehicles page 63

autotreno	**1**	transporter
pullman	**2**	coach (*US* bus)
autobotte	**3**	tanker (*US* fuel truck)
camion/autocarro	**4**	lorry (*US* truck)
furgone	**5**	van
betoniera	**6**	cement-mixer (*US* cement truck)
furgoncino	**7**	pick-up truck
carrello elevatore	**8**	fork-lift truck
roulotte	**9**	caravan (*US* trailer)
fuoristrada	**10**	jeep
macchina sportiva	**11**	sports car
berlina	**12**	saloon (*US* sedan)
decappottabile	**13**	convertible
familiare	**14**	estate (*US* station wago
utilitaria	**15**	hatchback

stazione di rifornimento	**1** filling-station
	(*US also* gas station)
specchio retrovisore esterno	**2** wing mirror
	(*US* side mirror)
indicatore di direzione	**3** indicator (*US* turn signal)
faro anteriore	**4** headlight
targa	**5** number-plate
	(*US* license plate)
tubo di scarico	**6** exhaust-pipe
paraurti	**7** bumper
fanale posteriore	**8** rear-light (*US* taillight)
bagagliaio	**9** boot (*US* trunk)
tergicristallo posteriore	**10** rear windscreen wiper
	(*US* rear windshield wiper)
pompa della benzina	**11** petrol pump (*US* gas pump)
tubo flessibile	**12** hose
ugello	**13** nozzle
cofano	**14** bonnet (*US* hood)
motore	**15** engine
filtro dell'aria	**16** air filter
testata del motore	**17** cylinder head
griglia del radiatore	**18** radiator grille

parabrezza	**19** windscreen (*US* windshield)
cruscotto	**20** dashboard
leva del cambio	**21** gear lever (*US* gearshift)
volante	**22** steering-wheel
indicatore del carburante	**23** fuel gauge
	(*US also* gas gauge)
tachimetro	**24** speedometer
accensione	**25** ignition
(pedale della) frizione	**26** clutch
(pedale del) freno	**27** footbrake
(pedale) acceleratore	**28** accelerator
	(*US also* gas pedal)

Bikes page 65

bicicletta	**1**	bicycle/bike
sella	**2**	saddle (*esp US* seat)
pompa	**3**	pump
telaio	**4**	frame
pedivella	**5**	crank
lucchetto	**6**	lock
raggi	**7**	spokes
catena	**8**	chain
pedale	**9**	pedal
moltiplica	**10**	chain-wheel
valvola	**11**	valve
mozzo	**12**	hub
leva del cambio	**13**	gear lever
		(*US* gear changer)
catarifrangente	**14**	reflector
cavo	**15**	cable
leva del freno	**16**	brake lever

triciclo	**17**	tricycle
campanello	**18**	bell
manubrio	**19**	handlebar
ruota	**20**	wheel
scooter	**21**	scooter
parafango	**22**	mudguard (*US* fender)
sedile	**23**	seat
baule portaoggetti	**24**	top box (*US* top case)
motocicletta	**25**	motor cycle
		(*Brit also* motor bike)
comando del gas	**26**	accelerator/throttle
pneumatico	**27**	tyre (*US* tire)
motore	**28**	engine
ammortizzatori	**29**	shock absorbers

cabina di manovra	**1**	signal-box (*US* signal tower)
passaggio a livello	**2**	level crossing (*US* grade crossing)
locomotiva	**3**	engine
carrozza passeggeri	**4**	coach (*US* passenger car)

La metropolitana — **The Underground (*US* The Subway)**

indicatore d'uscita	**5**	exit sign
marciapiede/banchina	**6**	platform
binario	**7**	line(s) (*esp US* track)
treno	**8**	train
galleria	**9**	tunnel

Alla stazione — **At the Station**

biglietteria	**10**	ticket office (*US* ticket counter)
sportello	**11**	window
coda	**12**	queue (*US* line)
borsa	**13**	bag
valigia	**14**	suitcase
orario	**15**	timetable
zaino	**16**	rucksack (*esp US* backpack)
cartellone delle partenze	**17**	departures board (*US* departure board)
numero del binario	**18**	platform number (*US* track number)
bigliettaio	**19**	ticket-collector (*US* ticket taker)
passeggera	**20**	passenger
entrata (al binario 10)	**21**	entrance (to platform 10)
cancello	**22**	barrier (*esp US* gate)

At the Airport 1 page 67

Nel terminale	In the terminal
accettazione	**1** check-in
biglietto aereo	**2** airline ticket
carta d'imbarco	**3** boarding pass
banco dell'accettazione	**4** check-in desk (*US* check-in counter)
controllo passaporti	**5** passport control
passaporto	**6** passport
misure di sicurezza	**7** security
rivelatore di metalli	**8** metal detector
rivelatore a raggi-X	**9** X-ray scanner
negozio esente da dazio	**10** duty-free shop
profumo	**11** perfume
sala delle partenze	**12** departures lounge (*US* departure lounge, waiting area)
posto a sedere	**13** seat
assistente di volo	**14** steward (*US* flight attendant)
uscita	**15** gate
ritiro bagagli	**16** luggage reclaim (*US* baggage reclaim)
bagaglio	**17** luggage
carrello	**18** trolley (*US* cart)
dogana	**19** customs
agente doganale	**20** customs officer

imbarco	**1** boarding	rotore	**10** rotor
passeggero	**2** passenger	pilota	**11** pilot
rimorchio	**3** trailer	aeroplano	**12** plane
	(*US* cart)	muso	**13** nose
torre di controllo	**4** control tower	cabina di pilotaggio	**14** cockpit
controllore del traffico aereo	**5** air traffic controller	elica	**15** propeller
decollo	**6** take-off	ala	**16** wing
pista	**7** runway	fusoliera	**17** fuselage
atterraggio	**8** landing	coda	**18** tail
elicottero	**9** helicopter	motore a reazione	**19** jet engine

barca a vela	**1** sailing-ship
albero	**2** mast
vela	**3** sail
ponte	**4** deck
cabina	**5** cabin
gomena	**6** cable (*US* line)
barca a remi	**7** rowing-boat (*US* rowboat)
remo	**8** oar
chiatta/barcone	**9** barge

porticciolo	**10** marina
motoscafo	**11** motor boat
panfilo/yacht	**12** yacht (*US also* sailboat)
cabinato	**13** cabin cruiser
peschereccio	**14** fishing boat
ormeggio/attracco	**15** mooring
prua/prora	**16** bow
poppa	**17** stern
battello di salvataggio	**18** lifeboat
canoa	**19** canoe (*US* kayak)
pagaia	**20** paddle

scalo/dock	**1**	dock
gru	**2**	crane
magazzino	**3**	warehouse
carico	**4**	cargo
nave	**5**	ship
petroliera	**6**	(oil-)tanker
aliscafo	**7**	hydrofoil
hovercraft	**8**	hovercraft
traghetto	**9**	ferry
fumaiolo	**10**	funnel (*US* smokestack)
nave di linea	**11**	liner (*esp US* ocean liner)
faro	**12**	lighthouse
scogli	**13**	rocks
gommone	**14**	inflatable dinghy (*US* rubber raft)
motore fuoribordo	**15**	outboard motor
ancora	**16**	anchor

Holidays 1 (*US* Vacations)

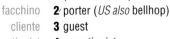
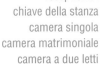

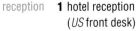

reception	**1**	hotel reception (*US* front desk)
facchino	**2**	porter (*US also* bellhop)
cliente	**3**	guest
receptionist	**4**	receptionist
chiave della stanza	**5**	room key
camera singola	**6**	single room
camera matrimoniale	**7**	double room
camera a due letti	**8**	twin room (*US* room with twin beds)
giro turistico	**9**	sightseeing
guida	**10**	tour guide
comitiva di turisti	**11**	party of tourists
turista	**12**	tourist
castello	**13**	castle
villa di campagna	**14**	country house
paese	**15**	village
la campagna	**16**	the countryside
picnic	**17**	picnic
campeggio	**18**	camping
tenda da campeggio	**19**	tent
telone impermeabile	**20**	groundsheet
sacco a pelo	**21**	sleeping-bag
fornello da campo	**22**	camping stove (*US* camp stove)
escursione a piedi	**23**	hiking
escursionista (a piedi)	**24**	hiker
zaino	**25**	rucksack (*esp US* backpack)
campeggio per roulotte	**26**	caravan site (*US* trailer camp)
roulotte	**27**	caravan (*US* trailer)

la spiaggia	**1**	the seaside
		(*esp US* the beach)
luogo di villeggiatura	**2**	holiday resort
spiaggia	**3**	beach
barriera marittima	**4**	sea wall
lungomare	**5**	promenade
		(*esp US* seafront)
crociera	**6**	cruise
lettino da spiaggia	**7**	sunbed
chi prende il sole	**8**	sunbather
ombrellone	**9**	sunshade
andare in barca a vela	**10**	sailing
vacanza in barca	**11**	boating holiday
		(*US* boating vacation)
canale	**12**	canal
pesca	**13**	fishing
pescatore	**14**	angler
canna da pesca	**15**	fishing-rod
andare a cavallo	**16**	pony-trekking
		(*US* horseback riding)
safari	**17**	safari
paracadutismo	**18**	parachuting
paracadute	**19**	parachute
viaggiare in mongolfiera	**20**	ballooning
mongolfiera	**21**	hot-air balloon
deltaplano	**22**	hang-gliding
deltaplano	**23**	hang-glider
alpinismo	**24**	climbing
alpinista/scalatore	**25**	climber
imbracatura	**26**	harness

The Environment page 73

montagna	**1**	mountain
vetta	**2**	peak
valle	**3**	valley
lago	**4**	lake
foresta	**5**	forest
cascata	**6**	waterfall
ruscello	**7**	stream
mare	**8**	sea
scogli	**9**	rocks
spiaggia	**10**	beach
scogliera	**11**	cliff
collina	**12**	hill
bacino idrico	**13**	reservoir
diga	**14**	dam
deserto	**15**	desert
sabbia	**16**	sand
duna	**17**	sand-dune
altopiano	**18**	plateau
bosco	**19**	wood (*esp US* woods)
fattoria	**20**	farm
casa colonica	**21**	farmhouse
fienile	**22**	barn
stagno	**23**	pond
campo	**24**	field
mietitrebbiatrice	**25**	combine harvester (*US* combine)
campo di grano	**26**	cornfield
grano	**27**	grain
trattore	**28**	tractor
aratro	**29**	plough (*esp US* plow)
solco	**30**	furrow

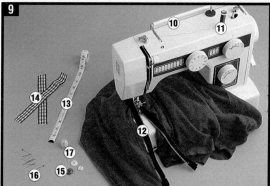
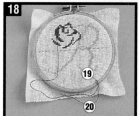

pittura	**1**	painting
disegno	**2**	drawing
ceramica	**3**	pottery
collezione di francobolli	**4**	stamp collecting
album per francobolli	**5**	stamp album
modellismo	**6**	making models
scatola di montaggio	**7**	kit
modello	**8**	model
cucito	**9**	sewing
macchina da cucire	**10**	sewing-machine
rocchetto di cotone	**11**	reel of cotton (*US* spool of thread)
cerniera	**12**	zip (*esp US* zipper)
metro a nastro	**13**	tape-measure
nastro	**14**	ribbon
bottone	**15**	button
spillo	**16**	pin
ditale	**17**	thimble
ricamo	**18**	embroidery
ago	**19**	needle
filo	**20**	thread
lavoro a maglia	**21**	knitting
lana	**22**	wool
ferro da calza	**23**	knitting-needle
tric trac/backgammon	**24**	backgammon
tavola	**25**	board
dama	**26**	draughts (*US* checkers)
shaker per dadi	**27**	shaker
dadi	**28**	dice
scacchi	**29**	chess
mazzo di carte	**30**	pack of playing-cards
fante di fiori	**31**	jack/knave of clubs
donna di cuori	**32**	queen of hearts
re di quadri	**33**	king of diamonds
asso di picche	**34**	ace of spades

Musical Instruments

page 75

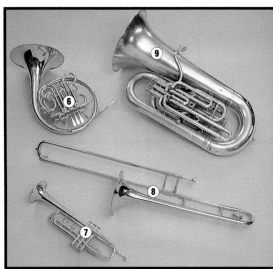
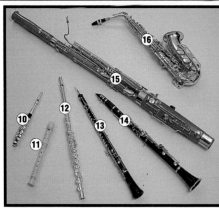

Archi	**Strings**
viola	**1** viola
archetto	**2** bow
violoncello	**3** cello
violino	**4** violin
contrabbasso	**5** (double-)bass
Ottoni	**Brass**
corno a pistoni	**6** French horn
tromba	**7** trumpet
trombone	**8** trombone
tuba	**9** tuba
Fiati	**Woodwind**
ottavino	**10** piccolo
flauto dolce	**11** recorder
flauto	**12** flute
oboe	**13** oboe
clarinetto	**14** clarinet
fagotto	**15** bassoon
sassofono	**16** saxophone
Percussioni	**Percussion**
timpano	**17** kettledrum
tamburello	**18** tambourine
bacchette per tamburo	**19** drumsticks
bongos	**20** bongos
piatti	**21** cymbals
conga	**22** conga
Altri strumenti	**Other instruments**
fisarmonica	**23** accordion
tastiera	**24** keys
armonica a bocca	**25** harmonica

Musica	**Music**
orchestra	**1** orchestra
musicista	**2** musician
pianoforte	**3** piano
direttore d'orchestra	**4** conductor
bacchetta	**5** baton
spartito musicale	**6** sheet music
complesso pop	**7** pop group
chitarra elettrica	**8** (electric) guitar
cantante	**9** singer/vocalist
tamburo/batteria	**10** drum
batterista	**11** drummer
tastierista	**12** keyboard player
sintetizzatore	**13** synthesizer
Il teatro	**The Theatre (*US* Theater)**
scenario	**14** scenery
palcoscenico	**15** stage
attore	**16** actor
attrice	**17** actress
quinte	**18** wings
fossa orchestrale	**19** orchestra pit
platea	**20** stalls (*US* orchestra seats)
galleria	**21** circle/balcony (*US* mezzanine)
loggione	**22** gallery (*US* balcony)
Il cinema	**The Cinema (*US* Movie Theater)**
schermo	**23** screen
stella del cinema	**24** film star (*US* movie star)
maschera	**25** usher
maschera	**26** usher (*Brit also* usherette)
corridoio	**27** aisle
pubblico	**28** audience

Sports 1

pattinaggio su ghiaccio	**1**	ice-skating
pattinare	**2**	skate (*verb*)
pattinatrice	**3**	skater
pattino da ghiaccio	**4**	ice-skate
pista di pattinaggio	**5**	ice-rink (*esp US* rink)
sci	**6**	skiing
sciare	**7**	ski (*verb*)
bastoncino	**8**	pole
sci	**9**	ski
sci acquatico	**10**	water-skiing
praticare lo sci acquatico	**11**	water-ski (*verb*)
chi pratica lo sci acquatico	**12**	water-skier
surf	**13**	surfing
onda	**14**	wave
fare surf	**15**	surf (*verb*)
surfista	**16**	surfer
tavola da surf	**17**	surfboard
windsurf	**18**	windsurfing
surfista	**19**	windsurfer
tavola a vela	**20**	sailboard
immersione subacquea	**21**	scuba-diving
bombola di ossigeno	**22**	(air)tank
nuoto con respiratore a tubo	**23**	snorkelling (*US* snorkeling)
respiratore a tubo	**24**	snorkel
nuoto	**25**	swimming
nuotare	**26**	swim (*verb*)
nuotatore	**27**	swimmer
piscina	**28**	swimming-pool
tuffarsi	**29**	dive (*verb*)
tuffatore	**30**	diver

baseball	**1**	baseball
caschetto del battitore	**2**	batting helmet
battitore	**3**	batter
guanto da baseball	**4**	baseball glove/mitt
maschera	**5**	face mask/catcher's mask
ricevitore	**6**	catcher
pubblico	**7**	crowd
pallacanestro	**8**	basketball
rete	**9**	net
tirare	**10**	shoot (*verb*)
football americano	**11**	American football
		(*US* football)
pallone	**12**	football
lanciare	**13**	throw (*verb*)
rugby	**14**	rugby
placcare	**15**	tackle (*verb*)
hockey su prato	**16**	hockey (*US* field hockey)
giocatore di hockey	**17**	hockey player
bastone da hockey	**18**	hockey stick
palla da hockey	**19**	hockey ball
pallavolo	**20**	volleyball
saltare	**21**	jump (*verb*)
squash	**22**	squash
racchetta	**23**	racket (*also* racquet)
gioco del volano	**24**	badminton
volano	**25**	shuttlecock
tennis da tavolo/ping-pong	**26**	table tennis
		(*esp US* ping-pong)
racchetta da ping-pong	**27**	table tennis bat
		(*US* paddle)
colpire	**28**	hit (*verb*)

Sports 3 page 79

freccette	**1** darts
bersaglio	**2** dartboard
mirare	**3** aim (*verb*)
biliardo	**4** snooker
stecca da biliardo	**5** cue
tavolo da biliardo	**6** table
buca	**7** pocket
bowling	**8** bowling
pista da bowling	**9** bowling-alley
birilli	**10** pins
golf	**11** golf
portamazze/caddie	**12** caddy
fairway/percorso normale	**13** fairway
green/piazzuola	**14** green
mazza da golf	**15** club
buca	**16** hole

pugilato	**17** boxing
angolo	**18** corner
quadrato	**19** ring
corde	**20** ropes
guantone da pugilato	**21** boxing glove
colpire con un pugno	**22** punch (*verb*)
lotta	**23** wrestling
lottare	**24** wrestle (*verb*)
arbitro	**25** referee
judo	**26** judo
karatè	**27** karate
spezzare	**28** chop (*verb*)

ginnastica	**1** gymnastics		atletica leggera	**15** athletics
ginnasta	**2** gymnast			(*US* track and field)
ciclismo	**3** cycling		campo	**16** field
andare in bicicletta	**4** cycle (*verb*)		pista	**17** track
automobilismo	**5** motor-racing		spettatori	**18** spectators
	(*US* auto racing)		corsia	**19** lane
pista automobilistica	**6** racetrack		atleta	**20** athlete
macchina da corsa	**7** racing car (*US* race car)		correre	**21** run (*verb*)
pilota di macchina da corsa	**8** racing driver		blocco di partenza	**22** starting-block
	(*US* race car driver)		ippica	**23** horse-racing
equitazione	**9** riding		correre	**24** race (*verb*)
	(*US* horseback riding)		cavallo da corsa	**25** racehorse
cavalcare	**10** ride (*verb*)		fantino	**26** jockey
cavallerizzo	**11** rider		cancello di partenza	**27** starting-gate
sella	**12** saddle		ippodromo	**28** racecourse
staffe	**13** stirrups			(*esp US* racetrack)
redini	**14** reins			

Tennis **Tennis**

incontro di singolo	**1** singles match
servire	**2** serve (*verb*)
chi serve	**3** server
linea di fondo	**4** baseline
linea di servizio	**5** service line
corridoio	**6** tramlines
	(*US* sidelines)
rete	**7** net
incontro di doppio	**8** doubles match
raccattapalle	**9** ballboy
campo da tennis	**10** tennis-court
arbitro	**11** umpire

Cricket **Cricket**

incontro di cricket	**12** cricket match
portiere	**13** wicket-keeper
battitore	**14** batsman
gambali	**15** pads
terreno tra le due porte	**16** pitch
lanciatore	**17** bowler
lanciare	**18** bowl (*verb*)
porta/paletti	**19** wicket/stumps
arbitro	**20** umpire
giocatore che rilancia la palla	**21** fielder
campo	**22** field

Calcio **Football**
(*esp US* Soccer)

segnare una rete	**23** scoring a goal
tribuna	**24** stand
guardalinee	**25** linesman
segnare	**26** score (*verb*)
palo della porta	**27** goalpost
porta/rete	**28** goal
mancare	**29** miss (*verb*)
portiere	**30** goalkeeper

Keeping Fit (*US* Keeping in Shape)

lanciare	**9**	throw (*verb*)
prendere	**10**	catch (*verb*)
dondolarsi	**11**	swing (*verb*)
fune	**12**	rope
arrampicarsi	**13**	climb (*verb*)
spalliera	**14**	wall bars
palestra	**15**	gym/gymnasium
volteggiare	**16**	vault (*verb*)
tappeto	**17**	mat
cavallo	**18**	vaulting-horse
stirarsi/tendersi	**19**	stretch (*verb*)
piegarsi all'indietro	**20**	bend over backwards (*verb*)
		(*US* bend over backward)
inginocchiarsi	**21**	kneel (*verb*)
flettersi	**22**	bend over (*verb*)
fischiare	**23**	blow a whistle (*verb*)
fischietto	**24**	whistle
fare la verticale	**25**	do a handstand (*verb*)
corda per saltare	**26**	skipping-rope
		(*US* jump rope)
saltare con la corda	**27**	skip (*verb*)

camminare	**1**	walk (*verb*)
correre/fare footing	**2**	jog (*verb*)
chi pratica il footing	**3**	jogger
...rsi sul materasso elastico	**4**	trampolining
cadere	**5**	fall (*verb*)
materasso elastico	**6**	trampoline
istruttore	**7**	instructor
rimbalzare	**8**	bounce (*verb*)

Verbs 1 page 83

Sta stirando/Sta stirando una camicia. **1** He is **ironing**/He's **ironing** a shirt.
Sta cucinando/Sta cucinando il pranzo. **2** He is **cooking**/He's **cooking** a meal.
Sta pulendo/Sta pulendo una finestra. **3** He is **cleaning**/He's **cleaning** a window.
Sta cucendo. **4** He is **sewing**.

Sta spazzando/Sta spazzando il vialetto. **5** He is **sweeping**/He's **sweeping** the path (*US also* walk).
Sta legando un sacco. **6** He is **tying up** a bag/He's **tying** a bag **up**.
Sta vangando/Sta vangando il terreno. **7** He is **digging**/He's **digging** the soil.
Sta arrotolando un tubo di gomma. **8** He is **winding up** a hose/He's **winding** a hose **up**.

Sta riempiendo un bollitore. **9** She is **filling** a kettle (*US* an electric teakettle).
L'acqua sta bollendo. **10** The water is **boiling**.
Sta versando l'acqua nella teiera. **11** She is **pouring** the water into a teapot.
Sta mescolando il tè. **12** She is **stirring** her tea.

 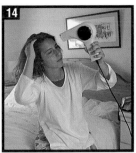  

Si sta lavando i capelli.	**13**	She is **washing** her hair.
Si sta asciugando i capelli.	**14**	She is **drying** her hair.
Si sta pettinando.	**15**	She is **combing** her hair.
Si sta spazzolando i capelli.	**16**	She is **brushing** her hair.

Sta sorridendo.	**17**	He is **smiling**.
Sta ridendo.	**18**	She is **laughing**.
Sta aggrottando le sopracciglia.	**19**	He is **frowning**.
Sta piangendo.	**20**	She is **crying**.

È seduto.	**21**	He is **sitting**.
È in piedi.	**22**	He is **standing**.
È disteso.	**23**	He is **lying down**.
Sta dormendo.	**24**	He is **sleeping**.

Verbs 3

Si stanno stringendo la mano.	**1** They are **shaking** hands.
Sta baciando la bambina.	**2** She is **kissing** the child.
Sta abbracciando la bambina.	**3** She is **hugging** the child.
Sta facendo cenno alla bambina.	**4** She is **waving** to the child.

Gli sta parlando.	**5** She is **speaking** to him/She is **talking** to him.
Stanno cantando.	**6** They are **singing**.
Stanno ballando.	**7** They are **dancing**.
Stanno applaudendo.	**8** They are **clapping**.

Gli sta dando un regalo.	**9** She is **giving** him a present.
Sta prendendo il regalo da lei.	**10** He is **taking** the present from her.
Sta aprendo il regalo.	**11** He is **opening** the present.
Sta leggendo il libro.	**12** He is **reading** the book.

Sta sollevando la valigia. **13** She is **lifting** the suitcase.
Sta portando la valigia. **14** She is **carrying** the suitcase.
Sta sorreggendo la valigia. **15** She is **holding** the suitcase.
Sta appoggiando la valigia. **16** She is **putting** the suitcase **down**.

Sta tagliando un pezzo di carta. **17** He is **cutting** a piece of paper.
Sta strappando un pezzo di carta. **18** He is **tearing** a piece of paper.
Sta piegando un pezzo di carta. **19** He is **folding** a piece of paper.
Sta spezzando una tavoletta di cioccolata. **20** He is **breaking** a bar of chocolate.

Sta spingendo un carrello. **21** She is **pushing** a trolley (*US* cart).
Sta tirando un carrello. **22** She is **pulling** a trolley (*US* cart).
Sta accendendo una candela. **23** He is **lighting** a candle.
La candela è accesa. **24** The candle is **burning**.

Contrastive Adjectives 1 page 87

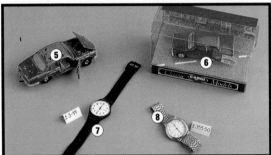

$$2 + 2 = 4 \qquad f(x) = \frac{1}{(x-4)(x+2)}$$

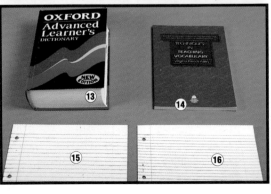

dritto	**1**	straight
storto	**2**	crooked
grande	**3**	big/large
piccolo	**4**	little/small
vecchio	**5**	old
nuovo	**6**	new
poco costoso	**7**	cheap
costoso	**8**	expensive
aperto	**9**	open
chiuso	**10**	closed
facile	**11**	easy
difficile	**12**	difficult
spesso	**13**	thick
sottile	**14**	thin
largo	**15**	wide
stretto	**16**	narrow
alto	**17**	high
basso	**18**	low
profondo	**19**	deep
basso/poco profondo	**20**	shallow
debole	**21**	weak
forte	**22**	strong
veloce	**23**	fast
lento	**24**	slow

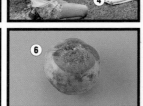

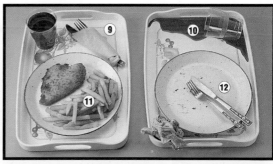

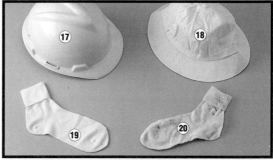

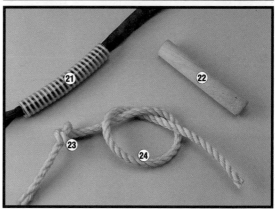

felice	**1**	happy
triste/infelice	**2**	sad/unhappy
rumoroso	**3**	loud
silenzioso	**4**	quiet
buono	**5**	good
cattivo	**6**	bad
ordinato	**7**	tidy (*esp US* neat)
disordinato	**8**	untidy (*esp US* messy)
asciutto	**9**	dry
bagnato	**10**	wet
pieno	**11**	full
vuoto	**12**	empty
leggero	**13**	light
pesante	**14**	heavy
ruvido	**15**	rough
liscio	**16**	smooth
duro	**17**	hard
morbido	**18**	soft
pulito	**19**	clean
sporco	**20**	dirty
vuoto	**21**	hollow
pieno	**22**	solid
stretto	**23**	tight
sciolto	**24**	loose

Animals 1 page 89

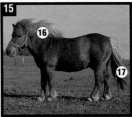

mucca	**1**	cow
vitello	**2**	calf
toro	**3**	bull
pipistrello	**4**	bat
riccio	**5**	hedgehog
scoiattolo	**6**	squirrel
volpe	**7**	fox
capra	**8**	goat
pecora	**9**	sheep
agnello	**10**	lamb
asino	**11**	donkey
zoccolo	**12**	hoof
cavallo	**13**	horse
puledro	**14**	foal
pony	**15**	pony
criniera	**16**	mane
coda	**17**	tail

Pets Animali domestici

gatto	**18**	cat			cane	**22**	dog
baffi	**19**	whiskers			cucciolo	**23**	puppy
pelo	**20**	fur			zampa	**24**	paw
gattino	**21**	kitten			criceto	**25**	hamster
					coniglio	**26**	rabbit

cervo	1	deer
corno ramificato	2	antler
lupo	3	wolf
orso	4	bear
artiglio	5	claw
orso polare	6	polar bear
panda	7	panda
canguro	8	kangaroo
marsupio	9	pouch
cammello	10	camel
gobba	11	hump
lama	12	llama
scimmia	13	monkey
gorilla	14	gorilla
zebra	15	zebra
leone	16	lion
tigre	17	tiger
leopardo	18	leopard
bufalo	19	buffalo
corno	20	horn
rinoceronte	21	rhinoceros
ippopotamo	22	hippopotamus
giraffa	23	giraffe
elefante	24	elephant
zanna	25	tusk
proboscide	26	trunk
foca	27	seal
pinna	28	flipper
delfino	29	dolphin
balena	30	whale

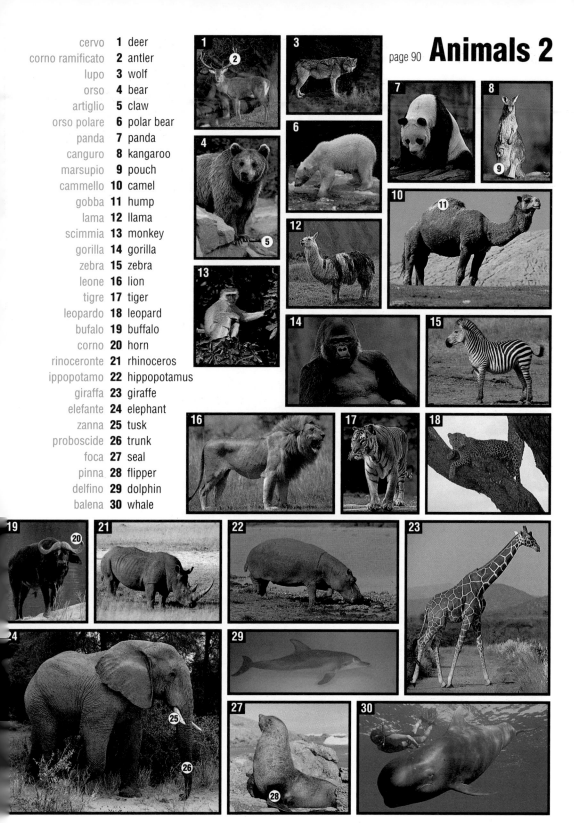

Fish and Reptiles page 91

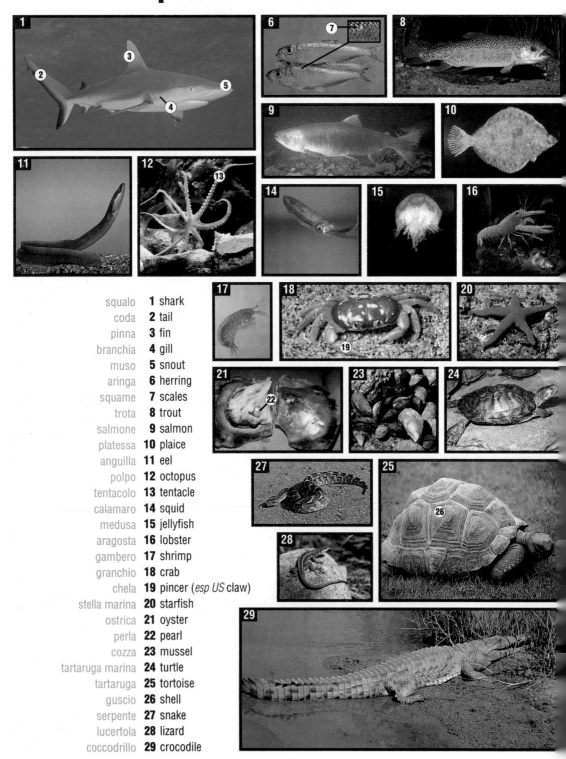

squalo	**1**	shark
coda	**2**	tail
pinna	**3**	fin
branchia	**4**	gill
muso	**5**	snout
aringa	**6**	herring
squame	**7**	scales
trota	**8**	trout
salmone	**9**	salmon
platessa	**10**	plaice
anguilla	**11**	eel
polpo	**12**	octopus
tentacolo	**13**	tentacle
calamaro	**14**	squid
medusa	**15**	jellyfish
aragosta	**16**	lobster
gambero	**17**	shrimp
granchio	**18**	crab
chela	**19**	pincer (*esp US* claw)
stella marina	**20**	starfish
ostrica	**21**	oyster
perla	**22**	pearl
cozza	**23**	mussel
tartaruga marina	**24**	turtle
tartaruga	**25**	tortoise
guscio	**26**	shell
serpente	**27**	snake
lucertola	**28**	lizard
coccodrillo	**29**	crocodile

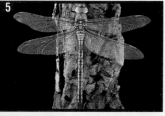

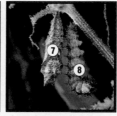

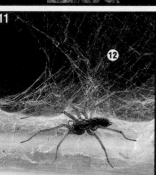

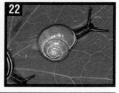

mosca	**1**	fly
ape	**2**	bee
vespa	**3**	wasp
zanzara	**4**	mosquito
libellula	**5**	dragonfly
farfalla	**6**	butterfly
bozzolo	**7**	cocoon
bruco	**8**	caterpillar
falena	**9**	moth
antenna	**10**	antenna
ragno	**11**	spider
ragnatela	**12**	(cob)web
scarabeo	**13**	beetle
coccinella	**14**	ladybird (*US* ladybug)
formica	**15**	ant
scarafaggio	**16**	cockroach (*also* roach)
cavalletta	**17**	grasshopper
grillo	**18**	cricket
mantide religiosa	**19**	praying mantis
lombrico	**20**	worm
lumaca	**21**	slug
chiocciola	**22**	snail
scorpione	**23**	scorpion
pungiglione	**24**	sting
rana	**25**	frog

Birds page 93

pollo	**1**	chicken
gallina	**2**	hen
pulcino	**3**	chick
gallo	**4**	cock (*US* rooster)
piuma	**5**	feather
tacchino	**6**	turkey
fagiano	**7**	pheasant
aquila	**8**	eagle
becco	**9**	beak
falco	**10**	hawk
corvo	**11**	crow
gufo	**12**	owl
nido	**13**	nest
piccione	**14**	pigeon
passero	**15**	sparrow
colibrì	**16**	hummingbird
ala	**17**	wing
canarino	**18**	canary
pappagallo	**19**	parrot
pappagallino	**20**	budgerigar (*US* parakeet)
rondine	**21**	swallow
struzzo	**22**	ostrich
pinguino	**23**	penguin
pavone	**24**	peacock
fenicottero	**25**	flamingo
becco	**26**	bill
oca	**27**	goose
anatra	**28**	duck
piede palmato	**29**	webbed foot
gabbiano	**30**	(sea)gull
cigno	**31**	swan

Simboli usati per la trascrizione fonetica

Vocali e dittonghi

1	iː	come in	**see** / siː /	11	ɜː	come in	**fur** / fɜː(r) /
2	ɪ	come in	**sit** / sɪt /	12	ə	come in	**ago** / əˈgəʊ /
·3	e	come in	**ten** / ten /	13	eɪ	come in	**page** / peɪdʒ /
4	æ	come in	**hat** / hæt /	14	əʊ	come in	**home** / həʊm /
5	ɑː	come in	**arm** / ɑːm /	15	aɪ	come in	**five** / faɪv /
6	ɒ	come in	**got** / gɒt /	16	aʊ	come in	**now** / naʊ /
7	ɔː	come in	**saw** / sɔː /	17	ɔɪ	come in	**join** / dʒɔɪn /
8	ʊ	come in	**put** / pʊt /	18	ɪə	come in	**near** / nɪə(r) /
9	uː	come in	**too** / tuː /	19	eə	come in	**hair** / heə(r) /
10	ʌ	come in	**cup** / kʌp /	20	ʊə	come in	**pure** / pjʊə(r) /

Consonanti

1	p	come in	**pen** / pen /	13	s	come in	**so** / səʊ /
2	b	come in	**bad** / bæd /	14	z	come in	**zoo** / zuː /
3	t	come in	**tea** / tiː /	15	ʃ	come in	**she** / ʃiː /
4	d	come in	**did** / dɪd /	16	ʒ	come in	**vision** / ˈvɪʒn /
5	k	come in	**cat** / kæt /	17	h	come in	**how** / haʊ /
6	g	come in	**got** / gɒt /	18	m	come in	**man** / mæn /
7	tʃ	come in	**chin** / tʃɪn /	19	n	come in	**no** / nəʊ /
8	dʒ	come in	**June** / dʒuːn /	20	ŋ	come in	**sing** / sɪŋ /
9	f	come in	**fall** / fɔːl /	21	l	come in	**leg** / leg /
10	v	come in	**voice** / vɔɪs /	22	r	come in	**red** / red /
11	θ	come in	**thin** / θɪn /	23	j	come in	**yes** / jes /
12	ð	come in	**then** / ðen /	24	w	come in	**wet** / wet /

/ ' / rappresenta *l'accento tonico principale* in parole come **about** / əˈbaʊt /
/ ˌ / rappresenta *l'accento secondario* in parole come **academic** / ˌækəˈdemɪk /

(r) Nella pronuncia dell'inglese britannico la 'r' racchiusa tra parentesi viene pronunciata solo quando ad essa segua un suono vocalico.
Nella pronuncia dell'inglese americano la 'r' non si omette.

Abbreviazioni britanniche ed americane

Brit motorway (*Brit*)
    sta ad indicare una voce usata solamente nell'inglese britannico

US zip code (*US*)
    sta ad indicare una voce usata solamente nell'inglese americano

    jug (*US pitcher*)
    sta ad indicare che una voce (jug) che è usata solamente nell'inglese britannico ha lo stesso significato del termine corrispondente (pitcher) che è usato unicamente nell'inglese americano

Brit also red (*Brit also* ginger)
    sta ad indicare che una voce (red) usata sia nell'inglese britannico che americano ha lo stesso significato di un termine corrispondente (ginger) che viene usato unicamente nell'inglese britannico

US also blackboard (*US also* chalkboard)
    sta ad indicare che una voce (blackboard) che è usata sia nell'inglese britannico che americano ha lo stesso significato di un termine corrispondente (chalkboard) che viene usato unicamente nell'inglese americano

esp US sofa (*esp US* couch)
    sta ad indicare che una voce usata principalmente nell'inglese britannico, ma che può anche essere usata nell'inglese americano (sofa), ha lo stesso significato di un termine ad essa corrispondente (couch) che è quello più comune nell'inglese americano

Index

Index

Index

Index page 105

Index

Indice generale

Indice generale

Indice generale

Indice generale

Indice generale

eople and Health Pages 1-8

Who's who?

Read the sentences about this family and then
write the names in the family tree.

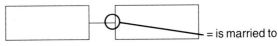
= is married to

Peter is married to Ann and they have a
daughter called Laura.
Peter's parents are Jack and Rosy.
Ann's sister, Sarah, has a son called Leo.

Linda is Ann's sister-in-law.
Alan's mother-in-law is called Joan.
Jamie is Leo's cousin.
Bill has got two grandsons and one granddaughter.

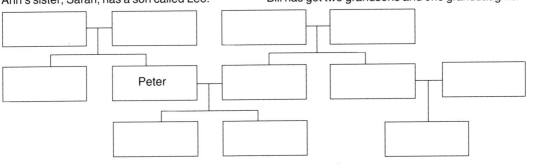

The Human Body

There are sixteen parts of the body hidden in this
square. Can you find them all?

e	i	b	h	e	a	d	e	n	o	x
o	y	u	e	a	m	o	o	a	t	s
t	o	e	o	u	b	i	f	i	s	t
a	e	z	o	m	e	f	i	l	o	o
n	c	a	u	e	c	a	n	g	e	m
k	e	h	i	e	a	h	g	i	i	a
l	t	e	i	o	u	e	e	i	o	c
e	e	a	o	n	a	i	r	s	e	h
u	l	u	o	e	t	x	u	e	t	e
a	i	b	a	c	k	a	e	e	i	e
e	p	a	i	k	n	e	e	t	e	k

What's the matter?

Match what the patient says to the doctor's advice.

Patient

a   I have dreadful earache.
b   I've got a sore throat and a temperature.
c   I've fallen over and hurt my arm.
d   I've got a small scratch on my leg.
e   I've got terrible toothache.

Doctor

1   Take two of these tablets and go straight to bed.
2   You probably need a filling.
3   Put two drops in each ear twice a day.
4   We'll need to put it in a sling.
5   Put some of this ointment on it and then cover it
    with a plaster.

a _3_   b ___   c ___   d ___   e ___

Exercises page 123

Clothes Pages 9-12

1 Test your memory!

Look carefully at page 10.

Fill in the missing words in the sentences below. Use words from the box.

a The woman is wearing a _____

blouse and a _____ blue jacket.

b The boy is wearing a _____

blazer and _____ trousers.

c The man is wearing a red and white

_____ tie and he is carrying a

raincoat.

d The girl is wearing a _____ coat

and a _____ scarf.

polka-dot	tartan	pink	grey	striped	plain	patterned

■ *Language note*

The man in the picture is **wearing** a suit and he is **carrying** a raincoat.

2 What other things are people carrying in the picture? Write some sentences.

_____

_____

_____

_____

_____

3 Match each of these words with the right part of the body.

trainer	head
belt	hand
watch	neck
glove	waist
tights	foot
helmet	legs
tie	wrist

4 Find the words from the mixed-up letters. They are all things that people wear or carry. When you have finished, read down the box to find the mystery word.

1. FRIEHCEKHDAN
2. FRASC
3. LABRUMEL
4. ERUPS
5. RECIFEABS
6. RENGIRA
7. LACKENCE
8. NABAHGD
9. GIRN
10. LOSECAHE
11. LAWLET
12. GESSNALUSS

1. h a n d k e r c h i e f
2. f
3. b
4. p
5. a
6. n
7. k
8. a
9. i
10. s
11. l
12. a

At Home Pages 15-22 and 58

Find the word in each group that is different from the others.

a   mug   cup   freezer   saucer   teapot

b   scales   aftershave   soap   shampoo   toothpaste

c   wardrobe   sideboard   vase   wall unit   chest of drawers

d   duster   brush   scourer   oven   mop

e   rake   watering-can   shears   lawnmower   bush

Write in the words.

a _____ **b** _____ **c** _____

d _____ **e** _____

f _____ **g** _____ **h** _____

Test your memory!

Look at page 18 for two minutes, then read these sentences about the picture. Decide if they are true or false.

a   The box of tissues is in the bedside cabinet.
b   There's a poster over the bed.
c   There's a hair-drier on the dressing table.
d   The dressing table is in front of the chest of drawers.
e   The blanket is under the bedspread.
f   There's a coat-hanger betweeen the light and the alarm clock.

If the sentences are false, write them correctly.

_____

_____

_____

_____

Exercises page 125

Shopping and Food Pages 23-28

1 Match a word in A with the right word in B.

A   B

a tube of   chocolate
a loaf of   cereal
a bar of   toothpaste
a bottle of   margarine
a jar of   jam
a packet of   bread
a tub of   biscuits
a box of   mineral water

2 Complete these dialogues using words from the box. Use each word only once.

1 a Can I help you?

   b Yes, please. How much are the

      _____ ?

   a They're 70p a bunch.

   b And the strawberries?

   a 85p a _____ .

2 a I'd like some _____

      for my wife's birthday.

   b Certainly, sir. Any particular kind?

   a Well, yes, she likes these blue ones.

   b Oh, you mean _____ .

3 a I'm looking for a _____

      of chocolates. Have you got any?

   b They're up on the top

      _____ .

   a They're a present for somebody so I'll

      need a roll of _____

      and a _____ of

      Sellotape too, please.

4 a Are you ready to order? Here comes the

      _____ .

   b No, I haven't decided yet. Are you going

      to have a _____ ?

   a Yes, I think I'll have the melon.

---

flowers bananas starter shelf punnet waiter wrapping paper irises box reel

3 Where do each of the conversations in exercise 2 take place?

1 _____   3 _____

2 _____   4 _____

Dates and Times Pages 33 and 37

1 Look at the clocks, then find two ways of saying each time, using the expressions in the box.

1 ___c,_____ 2 _____

 00:00

3 _____ 4 _____

5 _____ 6 _____

a	midnight
b	ten to five
c	eleven fifty-five
d	four fifty
e	a quarter to three in the afternoon
f	six thirty pm
g	seven minutes past four
h	two forty-five pm
i	half past six in the evening
j	twelve o'clock at night
k	five to twelve
l	four o seven

2 Dates

John always forgets important dates so he writes them down at the beginning of the year in a special page in his diary.

Look at the page, then answer the questions by writing the dates **in words**.

Important dates 1998

16/4 Mum's birthday

1/5 holiday (3 weeks)

3/8 Aunt Edna arrives from Australia

12/9 our wedding anniversary

22/11 – 30/11 exams!

a When is John's mother's birthday?

_____

b When does John's holiday begin?

_____

c On what date does Aunt Edna arrive?

_____

d When is John's wedding anniversary?

_____

e On what date do his exams finish?

_____

Exercises page 127

At Work Pages 39-40 and 43-44

1 What do we call someone who...

...reads the news aloud on the radio or TV?

_____

...arranges people's holidays for them?

_____

...works with wood?

_____

... makes bread and cakes?

_____

...treats sick animals?

_____

...repairs cars?

_____

2 Read these job advertisements and decide what job is being offered in each one.

a Ladies' and gentlemen's ***** needed for modern salon. Experience of cutting all types of hair necessary.

b ***** for long-distance deliveries. Must have licence.

c WANTED! Qualified ***** for small chemist's. Duties to include dispensing prescriptions plus general shop work.

d EXPERIENCE IN RADIO? Love all kinds of music? 'Joy FM' is looking for a *****.

a _____

b _____

c _____

d _____

3 Office wordsearch

There are thirteen words connected with the office in this square. Can you find them all?

e	a	n	d	i	s	k	a	i	l	s
i	o	c	h	e	q	u	e	o	e	i
u	b	o	i	e	s	y	f	u	t	w
f	c	t	t	a	i	k	d	n	t	a
t	i	e	y	u	n	r	i	g	e	a
e	u	l	p	e	e	r	a	c	r	i
i	e	i	e	l	p	u	r	d	x	x
n	g	r	p	i	u	o	y	a	e	u
e	c	a	o	o	i	e	f	m	i	o
s	t	e	o	x	p	u	u	o	y	e
s	n	o	t	e	b	o	o	k	a	e

cheque

_____

_____

_____

_____

_____

_____

_____

_____

_____

_____

_____

_____

Describing Things Pages 47-49 and 87-88

1 Write the names of these shapes.

a _____ b _____

c _____ d _____

e _____ f _____

■ *Language note*

We say: This page is **rectangular**.
(Not: **a rectangle**.)
Rectangular is an adjective.

Noun	Adjective
rectangle	rectangular
triangle	triangular
circle	circular
oval	oval
square	square
cylinder	cylindrical

2 Match these questions and answers by writing the correct number next to the questions.

Question

Answer

a What shape is it?

b How much does it weigh?

c How big is it?

d What's it made of?

e What's it used for?

1 It's used for measuring things and for drawing straight lines.

2 This one is made of plastic but they are also made of wood.

3 It's rectangular.

4 About 10g.

5 It's about 15 cm long, 3 cm wide and 0.2 cm thick.

What is it? It's on page 49 of this dictionary. _____

Find the opposites of these adjectives and write them in the puzzle.

1 crooked
2 thin
3 light
4 tight
5 empty
6 hollow
7 dry

Now read down the box to find another adjective!

3 h e a v y

Exercises page 129

The Weather Pages 51-52 and 56

1 **Look at the weather map of the British Isles below. Find a symbol for each of the words in the box and draw it.**

sun	cloud	rain
wind	fog	snow

■ *Language note*

The adjective from { **cloud** is **cloudy**. { **sun** is **sunny**.

Make adjectives from the other words in the box. (If you are not sure about the spelling, check on page 51.)

wind _____

snow _____

fog _____

rain _____

2 **Look at the weather map and write in the missing information below.**

Tomorrow's Weather

The South-East will start the day quite

(1)_____ and

(2)_____, but in the

South-West it's going to be rather

(3)_____ and

(4)_____. Further north it will

be (5) _____ all day with a

maximum (6)_____ of 7°C.

Over in Northern Ireland it will be

(7) _____ with some

(8)_____ during the morning and it

will be very (9) _____ on the coast.

Up in Scotland the temperature will fall to

(10) _____ 3°C and there may be

some (11)_____ .

The City Pages 57 and 59-60

---

1 **Letter-box or mailbox?**

These are six things that you can find in a city street. Complete the table by writing the British or American words.

British	American
letter-box	
	sidewalk
crossroads	
	traffic circle
	trash can
pedestrian crossing	

---

2 **Look at the pictures and complete the sentences using words from the box.**

a

b

c

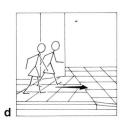
d

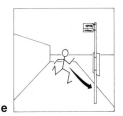
e

bus stop	building	pavement	across	away from
into	road sign	towards	along	road

a She is walking _____

the _____ .

b He is going _____ the

_____ .

c She is going _____ the

_____ .

d They are walking _____

the _____ .

e He is running _____

the _____ .

Exercises page 131

Travelling Pages 63-68

1   Label these pictures.

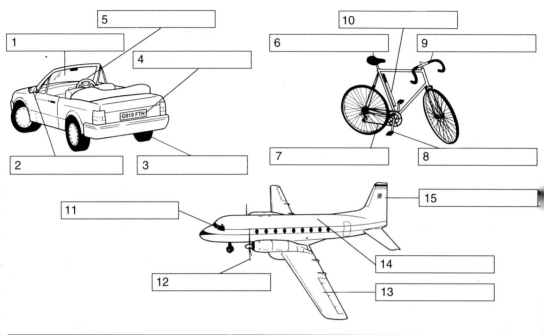

5		10
1	6	9
4		
2	7	8
3		
11	15	
12	14	
	13	

2   Airport crossword

Across

1   _____ pass

5

6   _____ desk
    (where you go to collect your *1 across*)

7

8   departure _____

10   You sit on this.

Down

2   _____ ticket

3   The part of the plane where the passengers are.

4   You can find an X-ray scanner here.

9   'Your flight is now boarding at _____ six.'

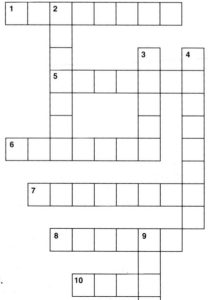

On Holiday Pages 71-73

Read the hotel information, look at the pictures, and fill in the missing words.

☀ Sunnyview Hotel - information

Please leave your [1] _ _ _ _ _ _ _ at the hotel reception when you go out.
Thank you.

★★★★★★★★★★★★★★★★★★★★★★★★★★★

Activities

Dalton Lake is only half a mile from the hotel. There you can go [2] _ _ _ _ _ _ _ or [3] _ _ _ _ _ _ _.

Northend-by-the-sea is a pretty holiday resort. Go [4] _ _ _ _ _ _ along the cliffs or just sit on the [5] _ _ _ _ _ and enjoy the sun!

If you want to do something really exciting, why not try [6] _ _ _ _ _ _ _ _ or even [7] _ _ _ - _ _ _ _ _ _?

★★★★★★★★★★★★★★★★★★★★★★★★★★★

SIGHTSEEING

Monday: Visit to Longleat, a historic [8] _ _ _ _ _ _ _ _ _ _ _ _ in Wiltshire.

Wednesday: A tour of the local countryside. A [9] _ _ _ _ _ _ is provided.

Friday: Coach trip to a beautiful [10] _ _ _ _ _ _ _ _ _ _ _.

Bring your camera!

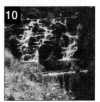

Music and Theatre Pages 75-76

1 Write the names of these instruments.
The words are in the box, but the letters of
each word have been mixed up.

a

b

c

d

e

f

tufel	olcel
phosanoex	bornmote
beamotunir	slycbam

2 What's the word?

a You walk along this to get to your seat in a
cinema or a theatre.

— — — — —

b He or she helps you to find your seat.

— — — — —

c Somebody who plays a large percussion
instrument.

— — — — — — —

d Where the orchestra sits.

— — —

e The American word for a 'balcony' in a
cinema or a theatre.

— — — — — — — — —

f Actors and actresses wait here before they
go on stage.

— — — — —

g A word that means 'singer'.

— — — — — — —

h Things on the stage of a theatre that make it
look like a real place.

— — — — —

Now take the first letter of each of the words you
found for **a**, **b** and **c**, the second letter of **d** and **e**
and the third letter of **f**, **g** and **h**. You will then
have the word for a group of people who are
watching a film or a play!

_____

Sports Pages 77-81

1 **Fill in the table using words from the box.**
Use each word only once.

Sport	Person	Place	Equipment
		court	
	caddy		
cricket			
		track	
			starting-gate

racket   athlete   jockey   club   horse-racing   stumps   starting-block   golf   field   racecourse   batsman   tennis   athletics   umpire   fairway

2 **Sports Quiz**

a   Name three sports in which players **tackle** each other.

b   What is the other name for **ping-pong**?

c   Name three objects that you need for playing baseball.

d   In which sport do players use **sticks**?

e   Name a sport that takes place under water.

f   Name three sports that need a **net**.

Exercises

Verbs Pages 83-86

---

1   What shall I do now?

Bob never knows what to do. Give him
some advice by writing the correct numbers by
the letters.

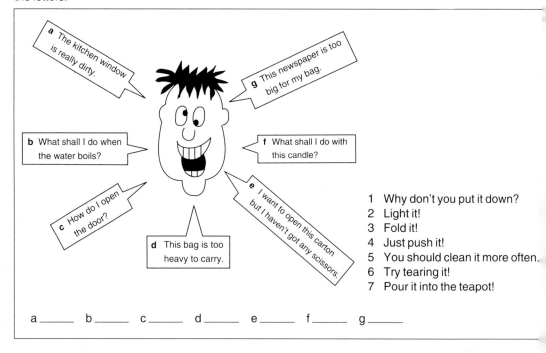

a The kitchen window is really dirty.

g This newspaper is too big for my bag.

b What shall I do when the water boils?

f What shall I do with this candle?

c How do I open the door?

e I want to open this carton but I haven't got any scissors.

d This bag is too heavy to carry.

1   Why don't you put it down?
2   Light it!
3   Fold it!
4   Just push it!
5   You should clean it more often.
6   Try tearing it!
7   Pour it into the teapot!

a _____   b _____   c _____   d _____   e _____   f _____   g _____

---

2   Match these verbs to the right thing or person.

You can...

cook   a friend
brush   a glass
dig   the drive
hug   your hair
shake   dinner
sweep   hands
fill   the soil

Animals

Pages 89-93

Wordsnake
Complete the puzzle with the first letter of each word at the correct number. Every answer except the first begins with the last letter of the word before it.

1   An insect with hard wings.

2   A large grey animal with a trunk.

3   A wild animal with yellow fur and black stripes.

4   It's got a horn on its nose.

5   This small animal has got a big tail and lives

   in trees.

6   A reptile with a long body usually seen in hot,

   dry places.

7   A young one of these is called a puppy.

8   It has a very long neck.

9   It looks like a snake and lives in water.

10 A young sheep.

11 A large black animal with horns found mainly

   in Asia and Africa.

12 It has got eight 'arms'.

13 We get wool from these.

14 A large animal with black and white fur.

15 A very small insect.

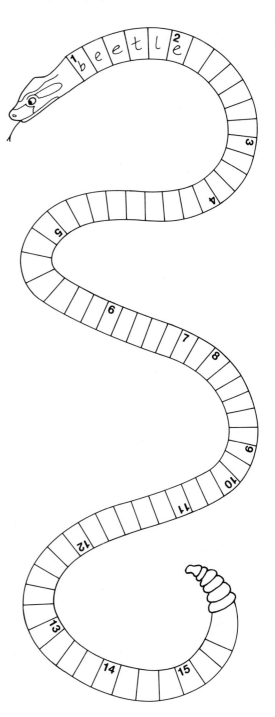

Key to exercises page 137

People and Health page 122

1
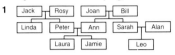

Jack	Rosy	Joan	Bill	
Linda	Peter	Ann	Sarah	Alan
	Laura	Jamie	Leo	

2 ankle, back, cheek, chest, chin, eye, finger, fist, head, knee, lip, nail, neck, stomach, toe

3 **b** 1 **c** 4 **d** 5 **e** 2

Clothes page 123

1 **a** patterned, plain **b** striped, grey
c polka-dot **d** pink, tartan

2 The girl is carrying an umbrella.
The woman is carrying a handbag and a briefcase.
The man is carrying a sweater.

3 belt - waist, watch - wrist, glove - hand, tights - legs, helmet - head, tie - neck

4 2. scarf 3. umbrella 4. purse
5. briefcase 6. earring 7. necklace
8. handbag 9. ring 10. shoelace
11. wallet 12. sun-glasses
dressing gown

At Home page 124

1 **a** freezer **b** scales **c** vase **d** oven
e bush

2 **a** frying-pan **b** plate **c** rolling-pin
d fork **e** ladle **f** kettle **g** jug
h toaster

3 **a** *false*. The box of tissues is on the bedside cabinet. **b** *true*. **c** *false*.
There's a hair-drier on the chest of drawers. **d** *false*. The dressing table is next to the chest of drawers. **e** *true*.
f *false*. There's a poster between the light and the alarm clock.

Shopping and Food page 125

1 loaf of bread, bar of chocolate, bottle of mineral water, jar of jam, packet of biscuits, tub of margarine, box of cereal

2 1. bananas, punnet 2. flowers, irises
3. box, shelf, wrapping paper, reel
4. waiter, starter

3 1. market 2. florist's 3. newsagent's
4. restaurant

Dates and Times page 126

1 1. c, k 2. f, i 3. g, l 4. a, j 5. b, d
6. e, h

2 **a** On the sixteenth of April/ April the sixteenth. **b** On the first of May/ May the first. **c** On the third of August/ August the third. **d** On the twelfth of September/ September the twelfth.
e On the thirtieth of November/ November the thirtieth.

At Work page 127

1 newsreader, travel agent, carpenter, baker, vet, mechanic

2 **a** hairdresser **b** lorry driver
c pharmacist **d** disc jockey

3 desk, diary, disk, fax, file, letter, notebook, pen, print, screen, stapler, type

Describing Things page 128

1 **a** circle **b** square **c** rectangle
d triangle **e** oval **f** cylinder

2 **a** 3 **b** 4 **c** 5 **d** 2 **e** 1 It's a **ruler**.

3 1. straight 2. thick 4. loose 5. full
6. solid 7. wet **shallow**

The Weather page 129

1
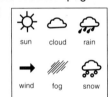

sun cloud rain

wind fog snow

windy snowy foggy rainy

2 1. cold 2. foggy 3. warm 4. sunny
5. cloudy 6. temperature 7. cool
8. rain 9. windy 10. minus
11. snow

The City page 130

1 mailbox, pavement, intersection, roundabout, litter-bin, crosswalk

2 **a** away from, road sign **b** across, road
c into, building **d** along, pavement
e towards, bus stop

Travelling page 131

1 1. windscreen 2. wing mirror 3. tyre
4. number-plate 5. steering-wheel
6. saddle 7. chain 8. pedal
9. handlebar 10. pump 11. cockpit
12. propeller 13. wing 14. fuselage
15. tail

2 1. boarding 2. airline 3. cabin
4. security 5. luggage 6. check-in
7. passport 8. lounge 9. gate
10. seat

On Holiday page 132

1. room key 2. sailing 3. fishing
4. hiking 5. beach 6. ballooning
7. hang-gliding 8. country house
9. picnic 10. waterfall

Music and Theatre page 133

1 **a** cello **b** trombone **c** flute
d tambourine **e** saxophone
f cymbals

2 **a** aisle **b** usher **c** drummer **d** pit
e mezzanine **f** wings **g** vocalist
h scenery **audience**

Sports page 134

1

Sport	Person	Place	Equipment
tennis	umpire	court	racket
golf	caddy	fairway	club
cricket	batsman	field	stumps
athletics	athlete	track	starting-blo
horse-racing	jockey	racecourse	starting-gat

2 **a** rugby, hockey, football
b table tennis
c batting helmet, baseball glove/mitt, face mask/catcher's mask
d hockey **e** scuba-diving
f basketball, volleyball, badminton, *or* tennis

Verbs page 135

1 **a** 5 **b** 7 **c** 4 **d** 1 **e** 6 **f** 2 **g** 3

2 brush your hair, dig the soil, hug a frie
shake hands, sweep the drive, fill a gl

Animals page 136

1. beetle 2. elephant 3. tiger
4. rhinoceros 5. squirrel 6. lizard
7. dog 8. giraffe 9. eel 10. lamb
11. buffalo 12. octopus 13. sheep
14. panda 15. ant